SELECTED POEMS II

Poems Selected & New 1976-1986

Margaret Atwood
SELECTED POEMS II
Poems Selected & New 1976-1986

Toronto Oxford University Press 1986

The poems reprinted in this collection are from
Two-Headed Poems, *True Stories*, and *Interlunar*,
published by Oxford University Press Canada,
and *Murder in the Dark*, published by Coach House Press.
New Poems have appeared in:
The Malahat Review
Exile
The Memphis State Review
Poetry Australia

CANADIAN CATALOGUING IN PUBLICATION DATA
Atwood, Margaret, 1939–
    Selected poems II
ISBN 0-19-540561-7
I. Title.
PS8501.T86A17 1986   C811'.54   C86-094625-8
PR9199.3.A87A17 1986

Printed in Canada by
Webcom Limited

Contents

Contents

Contents

From

TWO-HEADED POEMS

1978

BURNED SPACE

What comes in after a burn?
You could say nothing,

but there are flowers like dampened embers
that burst in cool white smoke

and after that, blue lights
among the leaves

that grow at the bases
of these blackened monoliths.

Before the burn, this was a forest.
Now it is something else:

a burn twists the green
eternal into singed grey

history: these discarded
stag-heads and small charred bones.

In a burn you kneel among the
reddish flowers and glowing seeds,

you give thanks as after a disaster
you were not part of,

though any burn
might have been your skin:

despite these liquid petals
against smoked rock, after a burn

your hands are never the same.

FORETELLING THE FUTURE

It doesn't matter how it is done,
these hints, these whispers:

whether it is some god
blowing through your head
as through a round bone
flute, or bright
stones fallen on the sand

or a charlatan, stringing you
a line with bird gut,

or smoke, or the taut hair
of a dead girl singing.

It doesn't matter what is said

but you can feel
those crystal hands, stroking
the air around your body
till the air glows white

and you are like the moon
seen from the earth, oval and gentle
and filled with light.

The moon seen from the moon
is a different thing.

A PAPER BAG

I make my head, as I used to,
out of a paper bag,
pull it down to the collarbone,

draw eyes around my eyes,
with purple and green
spikes to show surprise,
a thumb-shaped nose,

a mouth around my mouth
pencilled by touch, then coloured in
flat red.

With this new head, the body now
stretched like a stocking and exhausted could
dance again; if I made a
tongue I could sing.

An old sheet and it's Hallowe'en;
but why is it worse or more
frightening, this pinface
head of square hair and no chin?

Like an idiot, it has no past
and is always entering the future
through its slots of eyes, purblind
and groping with its thick smile,
a tentacle of perpetual joy.

Paper head, I prefer you
because of your emptiness;
from within you any
word could still be said.

With you I could have
more than one skin,
a blank interior, a repertoire
of untold stories,
a fresh beginning.

THE WOMAN WHO COULD NOT LIVE
WITH HER FAULTY HEART

I do not mean the symbol
of love, a candy shape
to decorate cakes with,
the heart that is supposed
to belong or break;

I mean this lump of muscle
that contracts like a flayed biceps,
purple-blue, with its skin of suet,
its skin of gristle, this isolate,
this caved hermit, unshelled
turtle, this one lungful of blood,
no happy plateful.

All hearts float in their own
deep oceans of no light,
wetblack and glimmering,
their four mouths gulping like fish.
Hearts are said to pound:
this is to be expected, the heart's
regular struggle against being drowned.

But most hearts say, I want, I want,
I want, I want. My heart
is more duplicitous,
though no twin as I once thought.
It says, I want, I don't want, I
want, and then a pause.
It forces me to listen,

and at night it is the infra-red
third eye that remains open
while the other two are sleeping
but refuses to say what it has seen.

It is a constant pestering
in my ears, a caught moth, limping drum,
a child's fist beating
itself against the bedsprings:

I want, I don't want.
How can one live with such a heart?

Long ago I gave up singing
to it, it will never be satisfied or lulled.
One night I will say to it:
Heart, be still,
and it will.

FIVE POEMS FOR DOLLS

i

Behind glass in Mexico
this clay doll draws
its lips back in a snarl;
despite its beautiful dusty shawl,
it wishes to be dangerous.

ii

See how the dolls resent us,
with their bulging foreheads
and minimal chins, their flat bodies
never allowed to bulb and swell,
their faces of little thugs.

This is not a smile,
this glossy mouth, two stunted teeth;
the dolls gaze at us
with the filmed eyes of killers.

iii

There have always been dolls
as long as there have been people.
In the trash heaps and abandoned temples
the dolls pile up;
the sea is filling with them.

What causes them?
Or are they gods, causeless,
something to talk to
when you have to talk,
something to throw against the wall?

A doll is a witness
who cannot die,
with a doll you are never alone.

On the long journey under the earth,
in the boat with two prows,
there were always dolls.

iv

Or did we make them
because we needed to love someone
and could not love each other?

It was love, after all,
that rubbed the skins from their grey cheeks,
crippled their fingers,
snarled their hair, brown or dull gold.
Hate would merely have smashed them.

You change, but the doll
I made of you lives on,
a white body leaning
in a sunlit window, the features
wearing away with time,
frozen in the gaunt pose
of a single day,
holding in its plaster hand
your doll of me.

v

Or: all dolls come
from the land of the unborn,
the almost-born; each
doll is a future
dead at the roots,
a voice heard only

on breathless nights,
a desolate white memento.

Or: these are the lost children,
those who have died or thickened
to full growth and gone away.

The dolls are their souls or cast skins
which line the shelves of our bedrooms
and museums, disguised as outmoded toys,
images of our sorrow,
shedding around themselves
five inches of limbo.

NOTHING NEW HERE

Nothing new here; just rain
in the afternoon, anger, two minutes of hail
that punched holes in the broad leaves;
then moist sun.

In the clearing air
we crouch in the garden, reconciled
for the moment, pulling out weeds.
Ragweed, pigweed, milkweed,
we know the names by now.
This is the fifth year.

Nothing stays free, though on what ought
to be the lawn, thistles blossom, their flowers
as purple as if I'd bought them;
around the edges of our cage,
outside the wire, there's the dying
rose hedge the mice ate.

What defeats us, as always, is
the repetition: weather
we can't help, habits we don't break.
The frogs, with their dud guitar-
string throats, every spring, release
their songs of love, while slugs breed
in the rain under the hay
we use for barricades;
milkweed and pigweed, the purslane
spreading its fleshy
starfish at our feet,
grabbing for space.

We know the names by now;
will that make anything better?
Our love is clumsier
each year, words knot
and harden, grow sideways, devious as grass.

Admit it,
this is what we have made,
this ragged place, an order
gone to seed, the battered plants
slump in the tangled rows,
their stems and damp rope sagging.
Our blunted fingers,
our mouths taste
of the same earth, bitter and deep.
(Though this is also what we have
in common; this broken
garden, measure
of our neglect and failure, still
gives what we eat.)

DAYBOOKS I

1

This is the somewhere
we were always trying to get:
landscape
reduced to the basics:
rolling hills, rocks, running
water, burdocks, trees living and dead,
the gambler's potato acres
brown money stuck in rows.
On this high ground, one late
frost or month of sun
finishes him.

No rain for weeks now, dust
twists across the fields,
the thigh-high clover
with its blossoms of white spittle
is sucked back into the ground.

2

Midnight: my house rests
on arrowheads and toebones,
scraps of raw fur, a cellar
scooped from the trashgrounds
of whatever ancestors once also
passed through time here,
shedding themselves piecemeal
in their long trek to sunset.

Things we are leaving:
bushel baskets and broken glass,
a knitted hand squashed flat,
potatoes that sprout and rot,
a rubber foot.

In this leaking boat I sail downhill
from one day to the next.

3

Someone came here, blunted
several good ploughshares,
cursed the groundhogs and their
ankle-breaking burrows,
hauled rocks until he died,
bursting a vein
out of sight of the house.
He had no sons, or if he did
they went elsewhere.

Stonepile in the back field,
overgrown by lichens, purple
nightshade, spindly raspberry,
the frame and springs of a sleigh.

We inherited this cairn
he and some glacier raised
to no memory in particular.

In one week we unbuild him,
pillage his limestone, shale,
red granite, delicate fossils.

This is the rock garden.
In it, the stones
too are flowers.

The rocks will stay
where they are put, for the time
being.

4

Eleven and no moon, the power
dead again, full weight
of August presses against my ears
with its chirps and dry whispers.

Downstairs, my daughter sleeps
in her jungle of pastel animals

with their milky noses and missing eyes;
green leaves are rising around her cage,
rubbery and huge, where she hunts and snuffles
on all fours through the hours;
she has eaten the eyes of the lion
and is the lion.

I stand in the upstairs hall
groping for stairwell; cat feet drip
through the darkness, threading the labyrinth
toward the sound of water.

What is there to dread, where
are the candles? My heart jumps
in the end of my left thumb,
small as a grape.

There is nothing to do but try
for courage, one stair and then
the next and hope
for vision, fearing

I have gone blind
but don't yet know it.

(I write this later, waiting
for the real thing.)

5

LETTERS

Almost winter, and in the gravel drive-
way under the stripped trees

a stack of dried voices clamouring
for replies. What can I tell you? That I

no longer live here?

I do not know
the manner of your deaths, daily
or final, blood
will not flow in the fossil

heart at my command, I can't
put the life back into those
lives, those lies. I know

where I live and it is not
in this box. If you need
the elixir of love
from me, you need
more than anyone can give.

As for the questions: How
am I? Can I, could I?
I can't, I never could;
I am / not.

6

AFTER JAYNES

The old queen's head cut off
at the neck, then skinned & emptied,
boiled, coated with plaster,
cheeks and lips dyed red,
bright stones in the eyes

    After this transformation
    she can sing,
    can tell us what we think
    we need to hear

    This is 'poetry', this song
    of the wind across teeth,
    this message from the flayed tongue
    to the flayed ear

7

November, the empty month; we try
to fill it with the smells
of cooking earth: baked roots, the comfort
of windfall pears, potatoes
floury and round, onions
& vinegar simmer

on the black stove, & the air
fogs with sugar; the risen bread says
this is where
we live,
            brave statement.

At night we make a fire
not for the warmth so much as for
the light
            & the old pumpkin
            lantern, our emblem,
            burns and shrivels, falling
            in upon itself, a gaunt
            sun, end
            of this year.

FIVE POEMS FOR GRANDMOTHERS

i

In the house on the cliff
by the ocean, there is still a shell
bigger and lighter than your head, though now
you can hardly lift it.

It was once filled with whispers;
it was once a horn
you could blow like a shaman
conjuring the year,
and your children would come running.

You've forgotten you did that,
you've forgotten the names of the children
who in any case no longer run,
and the ocean has retreated
leaving a difficult beach of grey stones
you are afraid to walk on.

The shell is now a cave
which opens for you alone.
It is still filled with whispers
which escape into the room,
even though you turn it mouth down.

This is your house, this is the picture
of your misty husband, these are your children, webbed
and doubled. This is the shell,
which is hard, which is still there,
solid under the hand, which mourns, which offers
itself, a narrow journey
along its hallways of cold pearl
down the cliff into the sea.

ii

It is not the things themselves
that are lost, but their use and handling.

The ladder first; the beach;
the storm windows, the carpets;

The dishes, washed daily
for so many years the pattern
has faded; the floor, the stairs, your own
arms and feet whose work
you thought defined you;

The hairbrush, the oil stove
with its many failures,
the apple tree and the barrels
in the cellar for the apples,
the flesh of apples; the judging
of the flesh, the recipes
in tiny brownish writing
with the names of those who passed them
from hand to hand: Gladys,
Lorna, Winnie, Jean.

If you could only have them back
or remember who they were

iii

How little I know
about you finally:

The time you stood
in the nineteenth century
on Yonge Street, a thousand
miles from home, with a brown purse
and a man stole it.

Six children, five who lived.
She never said anything
about those births and the one death;
her mouth closed on a pain
that could neither be told nor ignored.

She used to have such a sense of fun.
Now girls, she would say
when we would tease her.
Her anger though, why
that would curl your hair,
though she never swore.
The worst thing she could say was:
Don't be foolish.

At eighty she had two teeth pulled out
and walked the four miles home
in the noon sun, placing her feet
in her own hunched shadow.

The bibbed print aprons, the shock
of the red lace dress, the pin
I found at six in your second drawer,
made of white beads, the shape of a star.
What did we ever talk about
but food, health and the weather?

Sons branch out, but
one woman leads to another.
Finally I know you
through your daughters,
my mother, her sisters,
and through myself:

Is this you, this edgy joke
I make, are these your long fingers,
your hair of an untidy bird,
is this your outraged
eye, this grip
that will not give up?

iv

Some kind of ritual
for your dwindling,
some kind of dragon, small,
benign and wooden
with two mouths to catch your soul
because it is wandering
like a lost child, lift it back safely.

But we have nothing; we say,
How is she?
Not so good, we answer,
though some days she's fine.

On other days you walk through
the door of the room in the house
where you've lived for seventy years
and find yourself in a hallway
you know you have never seen before.

Midnight, they found her
opening and closing the door
of the refrigerator:
vistas of day-old vegetables, the used bone
of an animal, and beyond that
the white ice road that leads north.

They said, Mother,
what are you doing here?

Nothing is finished
or put away, she said.
I don't know where I am.

Against the disappearance
of outlines, against
the disappearance of sounds,
against the blurring of the ears
and eyes, against the small fears
of the very old, the fear
of mumbling, the fear of dying,
the fear of falling downstairs,
I make this charm
from nothing but paper; which is good
for exactly nothing.

v

Goodbye, mother
of my mother, old bone
tunnel through which I came.

You are sinking down into
your own veins, fingers
folding back into the hand,

day by day a slow retreat
behind the disk of your face
which is hard and netted like an ancient plate.

You will flicker in these words
and in the words of others
for a while and then go out.

Even if I send them,
you will never get these letters.
Even if I see you again,

I will never see you again.

THE MAN WITH A HOLE
IN HIS THROAT

The black hole in his throat
is the same as the black
holes in space.

He knows it only as
a quicksand of skin
above his collarbone,
an absence, a crater
at the base of his skull
into which, sooner
or later, everything falls:

His bed and the women
undulating within it,
his children, the squeezed bulb
of his heart, his shoes
and mended socks, which offer
the damp woollen comforts
of the mundane; even his laughter
which in its time bounced glasses
on the table: they are all
victims of that gradual swallow.

The hole in his throat
is hard to understand,
has never appeared, is not a wound;
to speak of filling it
or sealing it would be meaningless.
It is a personal
quirk, like a stammer
or a deformed foot,
and as relentless.

Nothing ever comes out of it,
he thinks, though sometimes words
emerge from it like oracles
or dead rabbits, and those
sitting at dinner sometimes
grow indistinct, tainted
with its darkness: have they been there?

The black hole in his throat
erodes him: around its edges
his flesh melts and vanishes.

To try to close it though
would be fatal: he needs his neck,
it keeps his head joined to that body
which night by night eludes him
like a horizon; which he still trusts.

In any case, the hole
in his throat is this: although
he does not own it, he
is its location,
he has been chosen.

He never speaks of it, he wears
high collars, his throat
holds this one secret well.

What could he say of it, this thumbnail
of nothing, this heavy cave
in himself, this numb spiral,
this miraculous pool
through which, when he looks in the mirror,
he can see the farthest stars?

MARRYING THE HANGMAN

She has been condemned to death by hanging. A man may escape this death by becoming the hangman, a woman by marrying the hangman. But at the present time there is no hangman; thus there is no escape. There is only a death, indefinitely postponed. This is not fantasy, it is history.

*

To live in prison is to live without mirrors. To live without mirrors is to live without the self. She is living selflessly, she finds a hole in the stone wall and on the other side of the wall, a voice. The voice comes through darkness and has no face. This voice becomes her mirror.

*

In order to avoid her death, her particular death, with wrung neck and swollen tongue, she must marry the hangman. But there is no hangman, first she must create him, she must persuade this man at the end of the voice, this voice she has never seen and which has never seen her, this darkness, she must persuade him to renounce his face, exchange it for the impersonal mask of death, of official death which has eyes but no mouth, this mask of a dark leper. She must transform his hands so they will be willing to twist the rope around throats that have been singled out as hers was, throats other than hers. She must marry the hangman or no one, but that is not so bad. Who else is there to marry?

*

You wonder about her crime. She was condemned to death for stealing clothes from her employer, from the wife of her employer. She wished to make herself more beautiful. This desire in servants was not legal.

*

She uses her voice like a hand, her voice reaches through the wall, stroking and touching. What could she possibly have said that would have convinced him? He was not condemned to death, freedom awaited him. What was the temptation, the

21

one that worked? Perhaps he wanted to live with a woman whose life he had saved, who had seen down into the earth but had nevertheless followed him back up to life. It was his only chance to be a hero, to one person at least, for if he became the hangman the others would despise him. He was in prison for wounding another man, on one finger of the right hand, with a sword. This too is history.

*

My friends, who are both women, tell me their stories, which cannot be believed and which are true. They are horror stories and they have not happened to me, they have not yet happened to me, they have happened to me but we are detached, we watch our unbelief with horror. Such things cannot happen to us, it is afternoon and these things do not happen in the afternoon. The trouble was, she said, I didn't have time to put my glasses on and without them I'm blind as a bat, I couldn't even see who it was. These things happen and we sit at a table and tell stories about them so we can finally believe. This is not fantasy, it is history, there is more than one hangman and because of this some of them are unemployed.

*

He said: the end of walls, the end of ropes, the opening of doors, a field, the wind, a house, the sun, a table, an apple.

She said: nipple, arms, lips, wine, belly, hair, bread, thighs, eyes, eyes.

They both kept their promises.

*

The hangman is not such a bad fellow. Afterwards he goes to the refrigerator and cleans up the leftovers, though he does not wipe up what he accidentally spills. He wants only the simple things: a chair, someone to pull off his shoes, someone to watch him while he talks, with admiration and fear, gratitude if possible, someone in whom to plunge himself for rest and renewal. These things can best be had by marrying a woman who has been condemned to death by other men for wishing to be beautiful. There is a wide choice.

*

Everyone said he was a fool.
Everyone said she was a clever woman.
They used the word *ensnare*.

*

What did they say the first time they were alone together in
the same room? What did he say when she had removed her
veil and he could see that she was not a voice but a body and
therefore finite? What did she say when she discovered that
she had left one locked room for another? They talked of love,
naturally, though that did not keep them busy forever.

*

The fact is there are no stories I can tell my friends that will
make them feel better. History cannot be erased, although we
can soothe ourselves by speculating about it. At that time there
were no female hangmen. Perhaps there have never been any,
and thus no man could save his life by marriage. Though a
woman could, according to the law.

*

He said: foot, boot, order, city, fist, roads, time, knife.

She said: water, night, willow, rope hair, earth belly, cave, meat,
shroud, open, blood.

They both kept their promises.

FOUR SMALL ELEGIES

(1838, 1977)

i

BEAUHARNOIS

The bronze clock brought
with such care over the sea,
which ticked like the fat slow heart
of a cedar, of a grandmother,
melted and its hundred years
of time ran over the ice and froze there.

We are fixed by this frozen clock
at the edge of the winter forest.
Ten below zero.
Shouts in a foreign language
come down blue snow.

The women in their thin nightgowns
disappear wordlessly among the trees.
Here and there a shape,
a limp cloth bundle, a child
who could not keep up
lies sprawled face down in a drift
near the trampled clearing.

No one could give them clothes or shelter,
these were the orders.

We didn't hurt them, the man said,
we didn't touch them.

ii

BEAUHARNOIS, GLENGARRY

Those whose houses were burned
burned houses. What else ever happens
once you start?

        While the roofs plunged
into the root-filled cellars,

they chased ducks, chickens, anything
they could catch, clubbed their heads
on rock, spitted them, singed off the feathers
in fires of blazing fences,
ate them in handfuls, charred
and bloody.

        Sitting in the snow
in those mended plaids, rubbing their numb feet,
eating soot, still hungry,
they watched the houses die like
sunsets, like their own
houses. Again

those who gave the orders
were already somewhere else,
of course on horseback.

iii

BEAUHARNOIS

Is the man here, they said,
where is he?

        She didn't know, though
she called to him as they dragged her
out of the stone house by both arms
and fired the bedding.

He was gone somewhere with the other men,
he was not hanged, he came back later,
they lived in a borrowed shack.

A language is not words only,
it is the stories
that are told in it,
the stories that are never told.

He pumped himself for years
after that into her body
which had no feet
since that night, which had no fingers.
His hatred of the words
that had been done became children.

They did the best they could:
she fed them, he told them
one story only.

iv

DUFFERIN, SIMCOE, GREY

This year we are making
nothing but elegies.
Do what you are good at,
our parents always told us,
make what you know.

This is what we are making,
these songs for the dying.
You have to celebrate something.
The nets rot, the boats rot, the farms
revert to thistle, foreigners
and summer people admire the weeds
and the piles of stones dredged from the fields
by men whose teeth were gone by thirty

But the elegies are new and yellow,
they are not even made, they grow,
they come out everywhere,
in swamps, at the edges of puddles,
all over the acres
of parked cars, they are mournful
but sweet, like flowered hats
in attics we never knew we had.

We gather them, keep them in vases,
water them while our houses wither.

We make too much noise,
you know nothing about us,
you would like us to move away.

بحسن لخليفة

Come to our backyard, we say,
friendly and envious,
but you don't come.

Instead you quarrel
among yourselves, discussing
geneologies and the mortgage,
while the smoke from our tireless barbecues
blackens the roses.

iv

The investigator is here,
proclaiming his own necessity.
He has come to clean your heart.

Is it pure white,
or is there blood in it?

Stop this heart!
Cut this word from this mouth.
Cut this mouth.

     (Expurgation: purge.
      To purge is to clean,
      also to kill.)

For so much time, our history
was written in bones only.

Our flag has been silence,
which was mistaken for no flag,
which was mistaken for peace.

v

Is this what we wanted,
this politics, our hearts
flattened and strung out
from the backs of helicopters?

We thought we were talking
about a certain light
through the window of an empty room,
a light beyond the wet black trunks
of trees in this leafless forest
just before spring,
a certain loss.

We wanted to describe the snow,
the snow here, at the corner
of the house and orchard
in a language so precise
and secret it was not even
a code, it was snow,
there could be no translation.

To save this language
we needed echoes,
we needed to push back
the other words, the coarse ones
spreading themselves everywhere
like thighs or starlings.

No forests of discarded
crusts and torn underwear for us.
We needed guards.

قلوبنا الآن أعلام (راايات)

Our hearts are flags now,
they wave at the end of each
machine we can stick them on.
Anyone can understand them.

They inspire pride,
they inspire slogans and tunes
you can dance to, they are redder than ever.

vi

Despite us
there is only one universe, the sun

burns itself slowly out no matter
what you say, is that

30

so?   The man
up to his neck in whitehot desert
sand disagrees.

                    Close your eyes now, see:
                    red sun, black sun, ordinary
                    sun, sunshine, sun-
                    king, sunlight soap, the sun
                    is an egg, a lemon, a pale eye,
                    a lion, sun
                    on the beach, ice on the sun.

Language, like the mouths
that hold and release
it, is wet & living, each

word is wrinkled
with age, swollen
with other words, with blood, smoothed by the numberless
flesh tongues that have passed across it.

Your language hangs around your neck,
a noose, a heavy necklace;
each word is empire,
each word is vampire and mother.

As for the sun, there are as many
suns as there are words for sun;

false or true?

vii

Our leader
is a man of water
with a tinfoil skin.

He has two voices,
therefore two heads, four eyes,
two sets of genitals, eight
arms and legs and forty
toes and fingers.
Our leader is a spider,

he traps words.
They shrivel in his mouth,
he leaves the skins.

Most leaders speak
for themselves, then
for the people.

Who does our leader speak for?
How can you use two languages
and mean what you say in both?

No wonder our leader scuttles
sideways, melts in hot weather,
corrodes in the sea, reflects
light like a mirror,
splits our faces, our wishes,
is bitter.

Our leader is a monster
sewn from dead soldiers,
a siamese twin.

Why should we complain?
He is ours and us,
we made him.

viii

If I were a foreigner, as you say,
instead of your second head,
you would be more polite.

Foreigners are not there:
they pass and repass through the air
like angels, invisible
except for their cameras, and the rustle
of their strange fragrance

but we are not foreigners
to each other; we are the pressure
on the inside of the skull, the struggle
among the rocks for more room,

the shove and giveway, the grudging love,
the old hatreds.

Why fear the knife
that could sever us, unless
it would cut not skin but brain?

ix

You can't live here without breathing
someone else's air,
air that has been used to shape
these hidden words that are not yours.

This word was shut
in the mouth of a small man
choked off by the rope and gold/
red drumroll
This word was deported

This word was gutteral,
buried wrapped in a leather throat
wrapped in a wolfskin

This word lies
at the bottom of a lake
with a coral bead and a kettle

This word was scrawny,
denied itself from year
to year, ate potatoes,
got drunk when possible

This word died of bad water.

Nothing stays under
for ever, everyone
wants to fly, whose language
is this anyway?

You want the air
but not the words that come with it:
breathe at your peril.

These words are yours,
though you never said them,
you never heard them, history
breeds death but if you kill
it you kill yourself.

What is a traitor?

x

This is the secret: these hearts
we held out to you, these party
hearts (our hands
sticky with adjectives
and vague love, our smiles
expanding like balloons)

, these candy hearts we sent you
in the mail, a whole
bouquet of hearts, large as a country,

these hearts, like yours,
hold snipers.

A tiny sniper, one in each heart,
curled like a maggot, pallid
homunculus, pinhead, glass-eyed fanatic,
waiting to be given life.

Soon the snipers will bloom
in the summer trees, they will eat
their needle holes through your windows

(Smoke and broken leaves, up close
what a mess, wet red glass
in the zinnia border,
Don't let it come to this, we said
before it did.)

Meanwhile, we refuse
to believe the secrets of our hearts,
these hearts of neat velvet,
moral as fortune cookies.

Our hearts are virtuous, they swell
like stomachs at a wedding,
plump with goodwill.

In the evenings the news seeps in
from foreign countries,
those places with unsafe water.
We listen to the war, the wars,
any old war.

xi

Surely in your language
no one can sing, he said, one hand
in the small-change pocket.

That is a language for ordering
the slaughter and gutting of hogs, for
counting stacks of cans. Groceries
are all you are good for. Leave
the soul to us. Eat shit.

In these cages, barred crates,
feet nailed to the floor, soft
funnel down the throat,
we are forced with nouns, nouns,
till our tongues are sullen and rubbery.
We see this language always
and merely as a disease
of the mouth. Also
as the hospital that will cure us,
distasteful but necessary.

These words slow us, stumble
in us, numb us, who
can say even Open
the door, without these diffident
smiles, apologies?

Our dreams though
are of freedom, a hunger
for verbs, a song
which rises liquid and effortless,

our double, gliding beside us
over all these rivers, borders,
over ice or clouds.

Our other dream: to be mute.

Dreams are not bargains,
they settle nothing.

This is not a debate
but a duet
with two deaf singers.

NASTURTIUM

Nasturtium, with all its colours
from old moon to cut vein,
flower of deprivation,
does best in poor soil,
can be eaten, adds
blood to the salad.

I can choose to enter
this room, or not to enter.
Outside, pile of sand,
pile of stones, thistles
pushing between them, cement
blocks, two discarded mattresses,
mounds of red clay.

The dead stand in the wheatfield,
unseen by all but one girl;
her clothing blows in the east wind,
theirs does not.

Inside, there is nothing
to speak of: a table, a chair.
The room does nothing,
but like a cave it magnifies.

The woman up the road
foretells the weather
from signs known only to her,
before an accident
can smell blood on the stairs.
Should this be cured?

On the floor, caked mud, ashes
left from the winter.
Matches, a candle
in a holder shaped like a fish.

This is the room where I live
most truly, or cease to live.

Nasturtium is the flower
of prophecy; or not,
as you choose.

SOLSTICE POEM

i

A tree hulks in the living-
room, prickly monster, our hostage
from the wilderness, prelude
to light in this dark space of the year
which turns again toward the sun
today, or at least we hope so.

Outside, a dead tree
swarming with blue and yellow
birds; inside, a living one
that shimmers with hollow silver
planets and wafer faces,
salt and flour, with pearl
teeth, tin angels, a knitted bear.

This is our altar.

ii

Beyond the white hill which maroons us,
out of sight of the white
eye of the pond, geography

is crumbling, the nation
splits like an iceberg, factions
shouting Good riddance from the floes
as they all melt south,

with politics the usual
rats' breakfast.

All politicians are amateurs:
wars bloom in their heads like flowers
on wallpaper, pins strut on their maps.
Power is wine with lunch
and the right pinstripes.

There are no amateur soldiers.
The soldiers grease their holsters,
strap on everything
they need to strap, gobble their dinners.
They travel quickly and light.

The fighting will be local,
they know, and lethal.
Their eyes flick from target
to target: window, belly, child.
The goal is not to get killed.

iii

As for the women, who did not
want to be involved, they are involved.

It's that blood on the snow
which turns out to be not
some bludgeoned or machine-gunned
animal's, but your own
that does it.

Each has a knitting needle
stuck in her abdomen, a red pincushion

heart complete with pins,
a numbed body
with one more entrance than the world finds safe,
and not much money.

Each fears her children sprout
from the killed children of others.
Each is right.

Each has a father.
Each has a mad mother
and a necklace of lightblue tears.
Each has a mirror
which when asked replies Not you.

iv

My daughter crackles paper, blows
on the tree to make it live, festoons
herself with silver.
So far she has no use
for gifts.

What can I give her,
what armour, invincible
sword or magic trick, when that year comes?

How can I teach her
some way of being human
that won't destroy her?

I would like to tell her, Love
is enough, I would like to say,
Find shelter in another skin.

I would like to say, Dance
and be happy. Instead I will say
in my crone's voice, Be
ruthless when you have to, tell
the truth when you can,
when you can see it.

Iron talismans, and ugly, but
more loyal than mirrors.

V

In this house (in a dying orchard,
behind it a tributary
of the wilderness, in front a road),
my daughter dances
unsteadily with a knitted bear.

Her father, onetime soldier,
touches my arm.
Worn language clots our throats,
making it difficult to say
what we mean, making it
difficult to see.

Instead we sing in the back room, raising
our pagan altar
of oranges and silver flowers:
our fools' picnic, our signal,
our flame, our nest, our fragile golden
protest against murder.

Outside, the cries of the birds
are rumours we hear clearly
but can't yet understand. Fresh ice
glints on the branches.
                              In this dark
space of the year, the earth
turns again toward the sun, or

we would like to hope so.

THE WOMAN MAKES PEACE
WITH HER FAULTY HEART

It wasn't your crippled rhythm
I could not forgive, or your dark red
skinless head of a vulture

but the things you hid:
five words and my lost
gold ring, the fine blue cup
you said was broken,
that stack of faces, grey
and folded, you claimed
we'd both forgotten,
the other hearts you ate,
and all that discarded time you hid
from me, saying it never happened.

There was that, and the way
you would not be captured,
sly featherless bird, fat raptor
singing your raucous punctured song
with your talons and your greedy eye
lurking high in the molten sunset
sky behind my left cloth breast
to pounce on strangers.

How many times have I told you:
The civilized world is a zoo,
not a jungle, stay in your cage.
And then the shouts
of blood, the rage as you threw yourself
against my ribs.

As for me, I would have strangled you
gladly with both hands,
squeezed you closed, also
your yelps of joy.
Life goes more smoothly without a heart,
without that shiftless emblem,
that flyblown lion, magpie, cannibal
eagle, scorpion with its metallic tricks
of hate, that vulgar magic,
that organ the size and colour

of a scalded rat,
that singed phoenix.

But you've shoved me this far,
old pump, and we're hooked
together like conspirators, which
we are, and just as distrustful.
We know that, barring accidents,
one of us will finally
betray the other; when that happens,
it's me for the urn, you for the jar.
Until then, it's an uneasy truce,
and honour between criminals.

MARSH, HAWK

Diseased or unwanted
trees, cut into pieces, thrown
away here, damp and soft in the sun, rotting and half-
covered with sand, burst truck
tires, abandoned, bottles and cans hit
with rocks or bullets, a mass grave,
someone made it, spreads on the
land like a bruise and we stand on it, vantage
point, looking out over the marsh.

Expanse of green
reeds, patches of water, shapes
just out of reach of the eyes,
the wind moves, moves it and it
eludes us, it is full
daylight. From the places
we can't see the gutteral swamp voices
impenetrable, not human,
utter their one-note
syllables, boring and
significant as oracles and quickly over.

It will not answer, it will not
answer, though we hit

it with rocks, there is a splash, the wind
covers it over; but
intrusion is not what we want,

we want it to open, the marsh rushes
to bend aside, the water
to accept us, it is only
revelation, simple as the hawk
which lifts up now against
the sun and into
our eyes, wingspread and sharp call
filling the head/sky, this,

to immerse, to have it slide
through us, disappearance
of the skin, this is what we are looking for,
the way in.

DAYBOOKS II

8

BLACK STONE MOTHER GOD

I chose from a lake's
edge, rests on the table
where I put her:
inert, all power
circled between thumb and finger.

From one side, an eye,
a head, a breast, a buttock.
From the other
a black potato,
a knob of earth, a long plum, a plump
elbow. A river shaped her,
smoothed her with sand and battered
her against the shore, and she
resisted, she is still here.

Worship what
you like, what you want
to be like . Old mother,
I pray to what is
and what refuses

9

You wanted to give me something:
a cactus. You said

I looked for one with flowers
but there weren't any.

The cactus sat in its pot.
of sand & stones, round
as a paperweight.
It did not grow or flower.

It could not be touched
without pain; finally

it could not be touched.

What was it you wanted
to say or offer?

Something different from what I have,
this clenched green apple, small

knowledge, thorny heart, this fist
shut against the desert air

(which however still guards
its one mouthful of water)

10

Every summer the apples
condense out of nothing
on their stems in the wet air
like sluggish dewdrops
or the tree bleeding.

Every fall they fall
and are eaten,
by us or something else,
wasps or snails, beetles,
the sandpaper mouths of the earth.

Every winter a few remain
on the branches, pulpy & brown,
wrinkled as kidneys or midget brains,
the only flesh in sight.

In spring we say the word *apple*
but it means nothing;
we can't remember those flavours,
we are blunt & thankless

But the apples condense again
out of nothing on their stems
like the tree bleeding; something
has this compassion.

11

APPLE JELLY

No sense in all this picking,
peeling & simmering
if sheer food is all
you want; you can buy it cheaper.

Why then do we burn our hours
& muscles in this stove,
cut our thumbs, to get these tiny
glass pots of clear jelly?

Hoarded in winter: the sun
on that noon, your awkward leap
down from the tree,
licked fingers, sweet pink juice,
what we keep
the taste of the act, taste
of this day.

12

How you disappear
in time, how you
disappear;

Who notices air?

Who could stand
a life all foreground?

Some days, yes, you fill
all the windows; some days you are
feverish and heavy, your bones
glow through the skin,
in winter even your shadow's
an ember on the floor;

But mostly this spring
you disappear
gradually into the sparse fringe
of willows on the other side
of the smokey pond,

into the dogwood; the melting snow
smudges your footprints

into
the not quite green

you disappear

Who notices air
except when it is gone

13

APRIL, RADIO, PLANTING, EASTER

In the air-
waves, on the contrary,
there is a lot of noise
but no good news

and there's a limit to how much
you can take of this battering
against the ears without imploding
like some land animal drifting down
into the blackout of ocean, its body
an eye crushed by pliers

so you fashion yourself a helmet
of thickened skin
and move cautiously among the chairs
prepared for ambush,
impervious to the wiry screams
and toy pain of the others.

But there is one rift, one flaw:
that vulnerable bud, knot,
hole in the belly where you were nailed
to the earth forever.

I do not mean *the earth*, I mean the
earth that is here and browns your
feet, thickens your fingers,
unfurls in your brain and in
these onion seedlings
I set in flats lovingly under
a spare window.

We do not walk on the earth
but in it, wading
in that acid sea
where flesh is etched from
molten bone and re-forms.

In this massive tide
warm as liquid
sun, all waves are one
wave; there is no *other*.

A RED SHIRT

For Ruth

i

My sister and I are sewing
a red shirt for my daughter.
She pins, I hem, we pass the scissors
back & forth across the table.

Children should not wear red,
a man once told me.
Young girls should not wear red.

In some countries it is the colour
of death; in others passion,
in others war, in others anger,
in others the sacrifice

of shed blood. A girl should be
a veil, a white shadow, bloodless
as a moon on water; not
dangerous; she should

keep silent and avoid
red shoes, red stockings, dancing.
Dancing in red shoes will kill you.

ii

But red is our colour by birth-

right, the colour of tense joy
& spilled pain that joins us

to each other. We stoop over
the table, the constant pull

of the earth's gravity furrowing
our bodies, tugging us down.

The shirt we make is stained
with our words, our stories.

The shadows the light casts
on the wall behind us multiply:

This is the procession
of old leathery mothers,

the moon's last quarter
before the blank night,

mothers like worn gloves
wrinkled to the shapes of their lives,

passing the work from hand to hand,
mother to daughter,

a long thread of red blood, not yet broken

iii

Let me tell you the story
about the Old Woman.

First: she weaves your body.
Second: she weaves your soul.

Third: she is hated & feared,
though not by those who know her.

She is the witch you burned
by daylight and crept from your home

to consult & bribe at night. The love
that tortured you you blamed on her.

She can change her form,
and like your mother she is covered with fur.

The black Madonna
studded with miniature

arms & legs, like tin stars,
to whom they offer agony

and red candles when there is no other
help or comfort, is also her.

iv

It is January, it's raining, this grey
ordinary day. My

daughter, I would like
your shirt to be just a shirt,
no charms or fables. But fables
and charms swarm here
in this January world,
entrenching us like snow, and few
are friendly to you; though
they are strong,
potent as viruses
or virginal angels dancing
on the heads of pins,
potent as the hearts
of whores torn out
by the roots because they were thought
to be solid gold, or heavy
as the imaginary
jewels they used to split
the heads of Jews for.

It may not be true
that one myth cancels another.
Nevertheless, in a corner
of the hem, where it will not be seen,
where you will inherit
it, I make this tiny
stitch, my private magic.

v

The shirt is finished: red
with purple flowers and pearl
buttons. My daughter puts it on,

hugging the colour
which means nothing to her
except that it is warm
and bright. In her bare

feet she runs across the floor,
escaping from us, her new game,
waving her red arms

in delight, and the air
explodes with banners.

NIGHT POEM

There is nothing to be afraid of,
it is only the wind
changing to the east, it is only
your father   the thunder
your mother   the rain

In this country of water
with its beige moon damp as a mushroom,
its drowned stumps and long birds
that swim, where the moss grows
on all sides of the trees
and your shadow is not your shadow
but your reflection,

your true parents disappear
when the curtain covers your door.
We are the others,
the ones from under the lake
who stand silently beside your bed
with our heads of darkness.
We have come to cover you
with red wool,
with our tears and distant whispers.

You rock in the rain's arms,
the chilly ark of your sleep,
while we wait, your night
father and mother,
with our cold hands and dead flashlight,
knowing we are only
the wavering shadows thrown
by one candle, in this echo
you will hear twenty years later.

ALL BREAD

All bread is made of wood,
cow dung, packed brown moss,
the bodies of dead animals, the teeth
and backbones, what is left
after the ravens. This dirt
flows through the stems into the grain,
into the arm, nine strokes
of the axe, skin from a tree,
good water which is the first
gift, four hours.

Live burial under a moist cloth,
a silver dish, the row
of white famine bellies
swollen and taut in the oven,
lungfuls of warm breath stopped
in the heat from an old sun.

Good bread has the salt taste
of your hands after nine
strokes of the axe, the salt
taste of your mouth, it smells
of its own small death, of the deaths
before and after.

Lift these ashes
into your mouth, your blood;
to know what you devour
is to consecrate it,
almost. All bread must be broken
so it can be shared. Together
we eat this earth.

YOU BEGIN

You begin this way:
this is your hand,
this is your eye,
that is a fish, blue and flat
on the paper, almost
the shape of an eye.
This is your mouth, this is an O
or a moon, whichever
you like. This is yellow.

Outside the window
is the rain, green
because it is summer, and beyond that
the trees and then the world,
which is round and has only
the colours of these nine crayons.

This is the world, which is fuller
and more difficult to learn than I have said.
You are right to smudge it that way
with the red and then
the orange: the world burns.

Once you have learned these words
you will learn that there are more
words than you can ever learn.
The word *hand* floats above your hand
like a small cloud over a lake.
The word *hand* anchors
your hand to this table,
your hand is a warm stone
I hold between two words.

This is your hand, these are my hands, this is the world,
which is round but not flat and has more colours
than we can see.

It begins, it has an end,
this is what you will
come back to, this is your hand.

NOTES

MARRYING THE HANGMAN
In eighteenth-century Quebec the only way for someone under sentence of death to escape hanging was, for a man, to become a hangman, or, for a woman, to marry one. Françoise Laurent, sentenced to hang for stealing, persuaded Jean Corolère, in the next cell, to apply for the vacant post of executioner, and also to marry her.

FOUR SMALL ELEGIES
After the failure of the uprising in Lower Canada (now Québec) in 1838, the British army and an assortment of volunteers carried out reprisals against the civilian population around Beauharnois, burning houses and barns and turning the inhabitants out into the snow. No one was allowed to give them shelter and many froze to death. The men were arrested as rebels; those who were not home were presumed to be rebels and their houses were burned.

The volunteers from Glengarry were Scots, most of them in Canada because their houses had also been burned during the Highland Clearances, an aftermath of the British victory at Culloden.   Dufferin, Simcoe, and Grey are the names of three counties in Ontario, settled around this period.

From
TRUE STORIES
1981

TRUE STORIES

i

Don't ask for the true story;
why do you need it?

It's not what I set out with
or what I carry.

What I'm sailing with,
a knife, blue fire,

luck, a few good words
that still work, and the tide.

ii

The true story was lost
on the way down to the beach, it's something

I never had, that black tangle
of branches in a shifting light,

my blurred footprints
filling with salt

water, this handful
of tiny bones, this owl's kill;

a moon, crumpled papers, a coin,
the glint of an old picnic,

the hollows made by lovers
in sand a hundred

years ago: no clue.

iii

The true story lies
among the other stories,

a mess of colours, like jumbled clothing
thrown off or away,

like hearts on marble, like syllables, like
butchers' discards.

The true story is vicious
and multiple and untrue

after all. Why do you
need it? Don't ever

ask for the true story.

LANDCRAB I

A lie, that we come from water.
The truth is we were born
from stones, dragons, the sea's
teeth, as you testify,
with your crust and jagged scissors.

Hermit, hard socket
for a timid eye,
you're a soft gut scuttling
sideways, a blue skull,
round bone on the prowl.
Wolf of treeroots and gravelly holes,
a mouth on stilts,
the husk of a small demon.

Attack, voracious
eating, and flight:
it's a sound routine
for staying alive on edges.

Then there's the tide, and that dance
you do for the moon
on wet sand, claws raised
to fend off your mate,
your coupling a quick
dry clatter of rocks.
For mammals
with their lobes and tubers,

scruples and warm milk,
you've nothing but contempt.

Here you are, a frozen scowl
targeted in flashlight,
then gone: a piece of what
we are, not all,
my stunted child, my momentary
face in the mirror,
my tiny nightmare.

LANDCRAB II

The sea sucks at its own
edges, in and out with the moon.
Tattered brown fronds
(shredded nylon stockings,
feathers, the remnants of hands)
wash against my skin.

As for the crab, she's climbed
a tree and sticks herself
to the bark with her adroit
spikes; she jerks
her stalked eyes at me, seeing

a meat shadow,
food or a predator.
I smell the pulp
of her body, faint odour
of rotting salt,
as she smells mine,
working those martian palps:

seawater in leather.
I'm a category, a noun
in a language not human,
infra-red in moonlight,
a tidal wave in the air.

Old fingernail, old mother,
I'm up to scant harm
tonight; though you don't care,

you're no-one's metaphor,
you have your own paths
and rituals, frayed snails
and soaked nuts, waterlogged sacks
to pick over, soggy chips and crusts.

The beach is all yours, wordless
and ripe once I'm off it,
wading towards the moored boats
and blue lights of the dock.

ONE MORE GARDEN

In the garden, waxy jasmine
& hibiscus jostle, the chaliceflower
one fat petal, a creamy orifice;
the punky stems
bulge visibly into fruit,
drop and are picked & sucked;
sex grows on trees, I told you.

Bananaquit, a squeal,
fingernail on blackboard,
at noon predictable,

and at dusk
slight pillowsmell of mildew,
the waterdrop of secret
green throats, their clear notes.

On bare feet, fishbelly
white, I wince
over stubble & around
sheepshit, to hang the wash.

The walls crack & sprout
ants & airy
lizards, varnish
peels off the ceiling, the sea is as blue
every morning as it always
was. In the salt air, hot

59

as tears, things manmade split & erode
as usual, but faster.

I should throw my gold watch
into the ocean and become
timeless. I'd stand more chance
here as a gourd, making
more gourds, as a belly
making more. Kiss your
thin icon goodbye, sink memory
& hope. Join the round
round dance. Fuck the future.

POSTCARD

I'm thinking about you. What else can I say?
The palm trees on the reverse
are a delusion; so is the pink sand.
What we have are the usual
fractured coke bottles and the smell
of backed-up drains, too sweet,
like a mango on the verge
of rot, which we have also.
The air clear sweat, mosquitoes
& their tracks; birds, blue & elusive.

Time comes in waves here, in sickness, one
day after the other rolling on;
I move up, it's called
awake, then down into the uneasy
nights but never
forward. The roosters crow
for hours before dawn, and a prodded
child howls & howls
on the pocked road to school.
In the hold with the baggage
there are two prisoners,
their heads shaved by bayonets, & ten crates
of queasy chicks. Each spring
there's a race of cripples, from the store
to the church. This is the sort of junk

I carry with me; and a clipping
about democracy from the local paper.

Outside the window
they're building the damn hotel,
nail by nail, someone's
crumbling dream. A universe that includes you
can't be all bad, but
does it? At this distance
you're a mirage, a glossy image
fixed in the posture
of the last time I saw you.
Turn you over, there's the place
for the address. Wish you were
here. Love comes
in waves like the ocean, a sickness which goes on
& on, a hollow cave
in the head, filling & pounding, a kicked ear.

NOTHING

Nothing like love to put blood
back in the language,
the difference between the beach and its
discrete rocks & shards, a hard
cuneiform, and the tender cursive
of waves; bone & liquid fishegg, desert
& saltmarsh, a green push
out of death. The vowels plump
again like lips or soaked fingers, and the fingers
themselves move around these
softening pebbles as around skin. The sky's
not vacant and over there but close
against your eyes, molten, so near
you can taste it. It tastes of
salt. What touches
you is what you touch.

SMALL POEMS FOR
THE WINTER SOLSTICE

1

A clean page: what
shines in you is not nothing,
though equally clear & blue

and I'm old enough to know
I ought to give up wanting
to touch that shining.

What shines anyway?
Stars, cut glass, and water,
and you in your serene blue shirt

standing beside a window
while it rains, nothing
much going on, intangible.

*

To put your hand
into the light reveals
the hand but the light also:
shining is where they touch.

Other things made of light:
hallucinations & angels.
If I reach my hands
into you, will you vanish?

2

Free fall
is falling but at least it's
free. I don't even know
whether I jumped or was pushed,
but it hardly matters now
I'm up here. No wings
or net but for an instant
anyway there's a great

view: the sea,
a line of surf, brown cliffs
tufted with scrub, your upturned
face a white zero.
I wish I knew
whether you'll catch or watch.

3

Mouth to mouth
I'm bringing you back to life.
Why did you drown like that
without telling?
What numbed you? What
rose over your head
was gradual and only
everybody's air,
standard & killing.
Your head floats on your hand,
on water, you turn
over, your heart returns
unsteadily to its two strong notes.
I'm bringing you back
to life, it's mutual.

4

Towards my chill house in this sloppy weather,
hands on the cold wheel, hoping there'll be a fire;
slush on the glass, past an accident,
then another. Somewhere there's one more,
mine. In a minuet we just
miss each other, in an accident
we don't. Dance is intentional but
did you miss me or
not, was it too close
to the bone for you, was that
pain, am I gone? Nothing's
broken, nevertheless I'm skinless,
the gentlest touch would gut me.
Slowly, slowly, nobody wants a mess.
I float over the black roads, pure ice.

5

No way clear,
I write on the lines across this yellow
paper. Poetry. It's details
like this that drag
at me, and the nasty little bells
on the corners I pass on my way
to meet you: singing of hunger,
darkness & poverty.

6

The weeks blink out, the winter solstice
with its killed pine branches
and tiny desperate fires
is almost upon us

again & again, in fifty versions:
the trees turn dull blue, the fields dun

for the last time.
We have a minute, maybe two

in which we're walking together
towards the edge of that evergreen forest
we'll never enter

through the drifted snow
which is no colour,
which has just fallen,

which has just fallen,
on which we will leave no footprints

7

This poem is mournful
& sentimental and filled
with complaints: where were you?
When I needed you.

I'd like to make
a bouquet of nice clean words for you,
hand it to you and walk away,
function accomplished. I can't
do it. This is the shortest day
of the year, shrunken,
blueveined & cold, deafmute.
That's me on the corner, sleet
down my neck, wordless. Where are you?

8

You think I live in a glass tower
where the phone doesn't ring
and nobody eats? But it does, they do
and leave the crumbs & greasy knives.

In the front room dogsmells
filter through the door,
dirty fur coats & the insides
of carnivore throats. Neglect
& disarray, cold ashes drift
from the woodstove onto the floor.
Cats with their melting spines festoon
themselves in every empty
corner. Who's fed them? Who knows?

What I want you to see
is the banality of all this, even
while I write the doorbell
pounds down there, constant assaults
of the radio, one more
blameless crushed face, another
pair of boots drips in the hall.

There's no mystery, I want to tell
you, none at all, no more
than in anything else. What I do
is ordinary, no
surprise, like you
no trickier than sunrise.

9

Some would say there's no excuse
for this collusion: while men
kill & mutilate each other, call it politics, burn
buildings & children, skewer
women through the eyes or bellies, we
hold hands in corner bars.

A distraction, takes your mind
off work or the jerky screen
where death is an event, love
isn't, unless it's double
suicide. How can I justify
this gentle poem then in the face of sheer
horror? A genteel pretence,
stupidity in this place of cracked
grey mud where the babies bloat
& wither and there's only one
quick exit from starvation.

Holding hands is a luxury
indulged in by the fat.
Still, if there were nothing
but killing or being killed then why not
kill? I know you by your
opposites. I know your absence.

10

Of course I'm a teller
of mundane lies, such as: I'll try
never to lie to you. Such as:
the day after today the earth will
tilt on its axis towards the sun
again, the light will turn stronger,
it will be spring and you'll
be happy. Such as:
I can fly. I wish I could believe
it. Instead I'm stuck
here, in this waste of particulars,
truths, facts. Teeth, gloves & socks.
I don't trust love
because it's no shape or colour.

11

I'd like you to be surprised
though, and greedy as a child
who does not need choices because all
choices are possible, and simple
as candy. A handful
of balloons, a grab and suddenly
you're in midair. Pure
delight, that's what you ought
to have, no difficult
chains & nets on your hands,
no tangled futures.

See, I hold out my hands to you,
lineless as if they'd been scalded,
wiped out. What innocence. Suppose I could do this,
would you want me to?

12

Afternoon: a wreck of paper
& coloured ribbons.
It rains & rains. You're as absent
as if unborn. Family swarms round us,
the machines hum:
clean dishes & music, dinner, steam
on the windows. What are you
up to? The same
things, I assume. The same dream.
Today you're the blank
side of the moon.

There's a cooked bird, a sharp knife:
that's real
and to be dealt with.

Arrogance, for me
to believe I know you
or anything about your life.

13

I'm in your hands, you say, meaning
something quite different: a way

of passing choice. Nevertheless
you're what I got handed,
not wanting it, like those cards
printed with the finger alphabet
the deaf & dumb nail you with in bus
stations. An embarrassment, but more
than that: some object
made of glass, lucid & simple
and without a name or known
function. I can learn you
by touch & guesswork
or not. Meanwhile I hold you
in my hands, true, wondering what
to make of you and what you'll make
of me. A gesture
of the hands, clear
as water. The letter A.

14

Is this really your fate,
to enter poetry and become transparent?

No ground under you, no feet or shoes,
no carpets, breadcrusts, calendars, no buttons,
pockets, hair, fur on the body, blood, unless
I put them there?

You're no good to me as a rumour,
blank & timeless. The year
isn't a clear circle or some
dream of a clock but one shadowy
moment after the next.
There's no choice, I have to take you
with all the clutter,
the fears, justified
or not, the smoky furniture,
dubious flesh, fatigue, the nagging
of daily voices, your obscure heart
neither of us can see, which beats
softly under my hand,
flying in darkness. Let's believe
you know your way.

TRUE ROMANCES

1

When I knew them they were an ordinary couple, she smiled and laughed a lot, she was a physiotherapist I think, and there was nothing wrong with him either, that you could see, except he was a little, you know. That summer they went on their vacation together, they always went on their vacation together, to Spain, that was back when you could still afford it, and everyone thinks he cut her up and left her in four garbage cans around the city, or maybe not in cans, do they have cans there? In Barcelona, except it wasn't Barcelona. It's like that guy who was keeping his wife in the freezer, you know? And a couple of kids went looking for some popsicles or whatever. He didn't even have a lock on the freezer, some people are pretty dumb. He said they'd gone to Madrid, except it wasn't Madrid, and one day she just went out for a walk and never came back, but the landlady, in Barcelona or whatever it was, says she saw him back at the flat or whatever it was they'd rented, after the day he said they'd gone to wherever. And the cans with her in them were in Barcelona, not Madrid. So they're there and he's here and naturally they want him to go over, for questioning they say, and naturally he won't. He says he doesn't need the distress all over again. I'll bet. Not that I would either if I was him. I saw him in the supermarket last week. He was holding an eggplant and he said, *Aubergine*, it's a much better word, don't you think? He was running his fingers over the purple skin. He hasn't changed a bit.

2

A long time ago I was desperately in love. Desperately is what I mean, in fact you could leave out the love and still get a good picture. He felt the same way and the strange thing was, neither of us could understand a word the other said. Because of this we used to throw dishes at one another, to attract each other's attention I suppose; we used to shout. For some reason they were always his dishes. Once I ran into his kitchen and cut a hole in my arm with his kitchen scissors, not a very big hole, so he could see there was real blood inside, but he didn't understand that either. It isn't sex that's the problem, it's language. Or maybe love makes you deaf, not blind, because now we go out to dinner every once in a while and we can understand each other perfectly, we tell jokes and we laugh at them, we really think they're funny. I look at him and I can't believe we once threw dishes at each other, but we did. I can remember which plates, which cups, which glasses, and which ones broke.

3

My friend called me on the telephone and said, I'm going to kill myself. Why? I said. He's left me, she said. I have nothing to live for. All right, I said, how are you going to do it? Pills? No, she said, that would make me sick. If it doesn't work, I mean. I can't stand having my stomach pumped out, it's humiliating. Well, a gun then, I said. Think of the mess, she said. It's indelible, and I hate loud noises. Hanging, I said. You look so awful, she said. You could say the same of drowning, I said. Well, I guess that's that, she said, but what am I going to do, now that he's left me and I have nothing to live for? Who told you it has to be for anything? I said. But were you living for him when he was there? No, she said. I was living in spite of him, I was living against him. Then you should say, I have nothing to live against, I said. It's the same thing, isn't it? she said. I said No.

4

Most people in that country don't eat eggs, she told me, they can't afford to; if they're lucky enough to have a chicken that lays eggs they sell the eggs. There is no such thing as *inside*, there's no such thing as *I*. The landscape is continuous, it flows through whatever passes for houses there, dried mud in and out, famine in and out, there is only *we*. That's why they can kill so many of us and not make any difference. To make a difference they would have to kill all of us. They cut off the hands and heads to prevent identification but they cannot prevent it. Everyone knows who has been shot and thrown into the sea, who has been beaten, which man or woman has been methodically raped, which left to starve and burn in a pit under the noon sun. It's bright there and clear, you can see a long way.

As for my lover, she told me, we had to separate. None of us can afford to live with just one other. You get careless, you forget how much you want to live, you start making bargains with yourself, you become dangerous to others. That kind of love is a weapon they can use against you. Among those of us who still have heads and hands there are no marriages.

5

I don't think about you as much as I ought to; I don't have to, you're there whether I think about you or not. Many people aren't.

When I do think about you it's not what you'd expect. I don't want to be with you: most of the time that would be an interruption, for both of us. I like to consider you going about your routine. I think about you getting up, brushing your teeth, having breakfast. I vary the breakfasts, though I don't devise anything too fanciful for you, I stick to cornflakes, orange juice, eggs, things like that. No strawberries out of season. I find it soothing to think about you eating these mundane and in fact somewhat austere breakfasts. It makes me feel safe.

But why should you go on eating breakfast at the same time, in the same way, day after day, just so I will be able to feel safe? You're contented enough, true, but there must be more. I'm getting around to that. One of these mornings, when you reach the bottom of your cup, coffee or tea, it could be either, you will look and there will be a severed finger, bloodless, anonymous, a little signal of death sent to you from the foreign country where they grow such things. Or you will glance down at your egg, four minutes, sitting in its dish white and as yet uncracked and serence as ever, and sunlight will be coming out of it. But on second thought your coffee cup will be vacant and the egg, when you finally close your eyes and slice it open blindly with the edge of your spoon, will have nothing in it that is not ordinarily there. Then you will know that at last I have imagined you perfectly.

Notes Towards a Poem
That Can Never Be Written

A CONVERSATION

The man walks on the southern beach
with sunglasses and a casual shirt
and two beautiful women.
He's a maker of machines
for pulling out toenails,
sending electric shocks
through brains or genitals.
He doesn't test or witness,
he only sells. My dear lady,
he says, You don't know
those people. There's nothing
else they understand. What could I do?
she said. Why was he at that party?

FLYING INSIDE YOUR OWN BODY

Your lungs fill & spread themselves,
wings of pink blood, and your bones
empty themselves and become hollow.
When you breathe in you'll lift like a balloon
and your heart is light too & huge,
beating with pure joy, pure helium.
The sun's white winds blow through you,
there's nothing above you,
you see the earth now as an oval jewel,
radiant & seablue with love.

It's only in dreams you can do this.
Waking, your heart is a shaken fist,
a fine dust clogs the air you breathe in;

the sun's a hot copper weight pressing straight
down on the thick pink rind of your skull.
It's always the moment just before gunshot.
You try & try to rise but you cannot.

THE ARREST OF THE STOCKBROKER

They broke the hands of the musician
and when despite that he would not stop singing
they shot him. That was expected.

You expected the poet hung upside down
by one foot with clothesline: in your head
you coloured his hair green. Art needs martyrs.

And the union leader with electrodes
clipped to the more florid
parts of his body, wired like
an odd zoological diagram:
if you don't keep your mouth shut
they'll choose the noise
you emit. Anyone knows that.
In some way he wanted it.

Reading the papers, you've seen it all:
the device for tearing out fingernails,
the motors, the accessories,
what can be done with the common pin.
Not to mention the wives and children.

Who needs these stories
that exist in the white spaces
at the edges of the page,
banal and without shape, like snow?

You flip to the travel ads; you're unable
to shake the concept of tragedy,
that what one gets
is what's deserved, more
or less; that there's a plot,

and innocence is merely
not to act.

Then suddenly you're in there,
in this mistake, this stage, this box,
this war grinding across
your body. You can't believe it.

Not only that, he's in here with you,
the man with the documents,
the forms, the stamps, the ritual prayers, the seals,
red & silver, and the keys, the signatures.

Those are his screams you hear,
the man you were counting on
to declare you legitimate:
the man you were always counting on
to get you out.

TORTURE

What goes on in the pauses
of this conversation?
Which is about free will
and politics and the need for passion.

Just this: I think of the woman
they did not kill.
Instead they sewed her face
shut, closed her mouth
to a hole the size of a straw,
and put her back on the streets,
a mute symbol.

It doesn't matter where
this was done or why or whether
by one side or the other;
such things are done as soon
as there are sides

and I don't know if good men
living crisp lives exist
because of this woman or in spite
of her.
            But power
like this is not abstract, it's not concerned
with politics and free will, it's beyond slogans

and as for passion, this
is its intricate denial,
the knife that cuts lovers
out of your flesh like tumours,
leaving you breastless
and without a name,
flattened, bloodless, even your voice
cauterized by too much pain,

a flayed body untangled
string by string and hung
to the wall, an agonized banner
displayed for the same reason
flags are.

FRENCH COLONIAL

For Son Mitchell

This was a plantation once,
owned by a Frenchman. The well survives,
filled now with algae, heartcoloured
dragonflies, thin simmer of mosquitoes.

Here is an archway, grown over
with the gross roots of trees,
here's a barred window,
a barn or prison.
Fungus blackens the walls
as if they're burned, but no need:
thickening vines lick over

and through them, a slow
green fire. Sugar,
it was then. Now there are rows
of yellowing limes, the burrows
of night crabs. Five hundred yards
away, seared women in flowered dresses
heap plates at the buffet.
We'll soon join them.
The names of the bays:
Hope, Friendship and Industry.

The well is a stone hole
opening out of darkness,
drowned history. Who knows
what's down there? How many
spent lives, killed muscles.
It's the threshold of an unbuilt
house. We sit on the rim
in the sun, talking
of politics. You could still
drink the water.

A WOMEN'S ISSUE

The woman in the spiked device
that locks around the waist and between
the legs, with holes in it like a tea strainer
is Exhibit A.

The woman in black with a net window
to see through and a four-inch
wooden peg jammed up
between her legs so she can't be raped
is Exhibit B.

Exhibit C is the young girl
dragged into the bush by the midwives
and made to sing while they scrape the flesh
from between her legs, then tie her thighs
till she scabs over and is called healed.

Now she can be married.
For each childbirth they'll cut her
open, then sew her up.
Men like tight women.
The ones that die are carefully buried.

The next exhibit lies flat on her back
while eighty men a night
move through her, ten an hour.
She looks at the ceiling, listens
to the door open and close.
A bell keeps ringing.
Nobody knows how she got here.

You'll notice that what they have in common
is between the legs. Is this
why wars are fought?
Enemy territory, no man's
land, to be entered furtively,
fenced, owned but never surely,
scene of these desperate forays
at midnight, captures
and sticky murders, doctors' rubber gloves
greasy with blood, flesh made inert, the surge
of your own uneasy power.

This is no museum.
Who invented the word *love*?

TRAINRIDE, VIENNA-BONN

i

It's those helmets we remember,
the shape of a splayed cranium,
and the faces under them,
ruthless & uniform

But these sit on the train
clean & sane, in their neutral
beige & cream: this girl smiles,

she wears a plastic butterfly, and the waiter gives
a purple egg to my child
for fun. Kindness abounds.

ii

Outside the windows the trees flow
past in a tender mist,
lightgreen & moist with buds

What I see though is the black trunks,
a detail from Breughel:
the backs of three men returning
from the hunt, their hounds following,
stark lines against the snow.

iii

The forest is no darker
than any forests, my own
included, the fields we pass
could be my fields; except
for what the eye puts there.

In this field there is a man
running, and three others, chasing,
their brown coats
flapping against their boots.

Among the tree roots the running man
stumbles and is thrown
face down and stays there.

iv

What holds me
in the story we've all heard
so many times before:

the few who resisted,
who did not do what they were told.

This is the old fear:
not what can be done to you

but what you might do
yourself, or fail to.

This is the old torture.

v

Three men in dark archaic
coats, their backs to me, returning
home to food and a good fire,
joking together, their hounds following.

This forest is alien
to me, closer than skin,
unknown, something early
as caves and buried, hard,

a chipped stone knife, the
long bone lying in darkness
inside my right arm: not
innocent but latent.

NOTES TOWARDS A POEM
THAT CAN NEVER BE WRITTEN

For Carolyn Forché

i

This is the place
you would rather not know about,
this is the place that will inhabit you,
this is the place you cannot imagine,
this is the place that will finally defeat you

where the word *why* shrivels and empties
itself. This is famine.

ii

There is no poem you can write
about it, the sandpits

where so many were buried
& unearthed, the unendurable
pain still traced on their skins.

This did not happen last year
or forty years ago but last week.
This has been happening,
this happens.

We make wreaths of adjectives for them,
we count them like beads,
we turn them into statistics & litanies
and into poems like this one.

Nothing works.
They remain what they are.

iii

The woman lies on the wet cement floor
under the unending light,
needle marks on her arms put there
to kill the brain
and wonders why she is dying.

She is dying because she said.
She is dying for the sake of the word.
It is her body, silent
and fingerless, writing this poem.

iv

It resembles an operation
but it is not one

nor despite the spread legs, grunts
& blood, is it a birth.

Partly it's a job,
partly it's a display of skill
like a concerto.

It can be done badly
or well, they tell themselves.

Partly it's an art.

v

The facts of this world seen clearly
are seen through tears;
why tell me then
there is something wrong with my eyes?

To see clearly and without flinching,
without turning away,
this is agony, the eyes taped open
two inches from the sun.

What is it you see then?
Is it a bad dream, a hallucination?
Is it a vision?
What is it you hear?

The razor across the eyeball
is a detail from an old film.
It is also a truth.
Witness is what you must bear.

vi

In this country you can say what you like
because no one will listen to you anyway,
it's safe enough, in this country you can try to write
the poem that can never be written,
the poem that invents
nothing and excuses nothing,
because you invent and excuse yourself each day.

Elsewhere, this poem is not invention.
Elsewhere, this poem takes courage.
Elsewhere, this poem must be written
because the poets are already dead.

Elsewhere, this poem must be written
as if you are already dead,
as if nothing more can be done
or said to save you.

Elsewhere you must write this poem
because there is nothing more to do.

VULTURES

Hung there in the thermal
whiteout of noon, dark ash
in the chimney's updraft, turning
slowly like a thumb pressed down
on target; indolent V's; flies, until they drop.

Then they're hyenas, raucous
around the kill, flapping their black
umbrellas, the feathered red-eyed widows
whose pot bodies violate mourning,
the snigger at funerals,
the burp at the wake.

They cluster, like beetles
laying their eggs on carrion,
gluttonous for a space, a little
territory of murder: food
and children.

Frowzy old saint, bald-
headed and musty, scrawny-
necked recluse on your pillar
of blazing air which is not
heaven: what do you make
of death, which you do not
cause, which you eat daily?

I make life, which is a prayer.
I make clean bones.
I make a grey zinc noise
which to me is a song.

Well, heart, out of all this
carnage, could you do better?

EARTH

It isn't winter that brings it
out, my cowardice,
but the thickening summer I wallow in
right now, stinking of lilacs, green
with worms & stamens duplicating themselves
each one the same

I squat among rows of seeds & imposters
and snout my hand into the juicy dirt:
charred chicken bones, rusted nails,
dogbones, stones, stove ashes.
Down there is another hand, yours, hopeless,
down there is a future.

in which you're a white white picture
with a name I forgot to write
underneath, and no date,

in which you're a suit
hanging with its stubs of sleeves
in a cupboard in a house
in a city I've never entered,

a missed beat in space
which nevertheless unrolls itself
as usual. As usual:
that's why I don't want to go on with this.

(I'll want to make a hole in the earth
the size of an implosion, a leaf, a dwarf
star, a cave
in time that opens back & back into
absolute darkness and at last
into a small pale moon of light
the size of a hand,
I'll want to call you out of the grave
in the form of anything at all)

SUNSET I

This is a different beach,
grudging & thin. Behind, the standard
industrial detritus. In front the generous
gasping sea, which flops against the shore
like a stranded flounder.
Tonight there's no crescendo
in the sun either, no brilliant red
catastrophes, no slashed
jugulars; merely a smudged egg.

We walk in our boots, too chilled
for skin on the sand, which is anyway
smeared with grease and littered
with exhausted lunches and clumps of torn-out
hair. There's a seagull,
avarice in its yellow
eye. It would like us face down
in the ebbtide. I hold your hand, which probably
detaches at the wrist. Heat theory states
I'll soon be as cold as you. Plato
has a lot to answer for.

I'd take you where
I'm going, but you won't come,
you're snowbound & numb & neatly
ordered. No remedy, drop everything,
wade into the illegal
greying sea, with its dirty
sacred water and its taste of dissolving metal,
which is nearly dead but still trying,
which is not ethical.

VARIATIONS ON THE WORD *LOVE*

This is a word we use to plug
holes with. It's the right size for those warm
blanks in speech, for those red heart-
shaped vacancies on the page that look nothing
like real hearts. Add lace
and you can sell
it. We insert it also in the one empty
space on the printed form
that comes with no instructions. There are whole
magazines with not much in them
but the word *love*, you can
rub it all over your body and you
can cook with it too. How do we know
it isn't what goes on at the cool
debaucheries of slugs under damp
pieces of cardboard? As for the weed-
seedlings nosing their tough snouts up
among the lettuces, they shout it.
Love! Love! sing the soldiers, raising
their glittering knives in salute.

Then there's the two
of us. This word
is far too short for us, it has only
four letters, too sparse
to fill those deep bare
vacuums between the stars
that press on us with their deafness.
It's not love we don't wish
to fall into, but that fear.
This word is not enough but it will
have to do. It's a single
vowel in this metallic
silence, a mouth that says
O again and again in wonder
and pain, a breath, a finger-
grip on a cliffside. You can
hold on or let go.

SUNSET II

Sunset, now that we're finally in it
is not what we thought.

Did you expect this violet black
soft edge to outer space, fragile as blown ash
and shuddering like oil, or the reddish
orange that flows into
your lungs and through your fingers?
The waves smooth mouthpink light
over your eyes, fold after fold.
This is the sun you breathe in,
pale blue. Did you
expect it to be this warm?

One more goodbye,
sentimental as they all are.
The far west recedes from us
like a mauve postcard of itself
and dissolves into the sea.

Now there's a moon,
an irony. We walk
north towards no home,
joined at the hand.

I'll love you forever,
I can't stop time.

This is you on my skin somewhere
in the form of sand.

VARIATION ON THE WORD *SLEEP*

I would like to watch you sleeping,
which may not happen.
I would like to watch you,
sleeping. I would like to sleep
with you, to enter
your sleep as its smooth dark wave
slides over my head

and walk with you through that lucent
wavering forest of bluegreen leaves
with its watery sun & three moons
towards the cave where you must descend,
towards your worst fear

I would like to give you the silver
branch, the small white flower, the one
word that will protect you
from the grief at the center
of your dream, from the grief
at the center. I would like to follow
you up the long stairway
again & become
the boat that would row you back
carefully, a flame
in two cupped hands
to where your body lies
beside me, and you enter
it as easily as breathing in

I would like to be the air
that inhabits you for a moment
only. I would like to be that unnoticed
& that necessary.

OUT

This is all you go with,
not much, a plastic bag
with a zipper, a bar of soap,
a command, blood in the sink,
the body's word.

You spiral out there,
locked & single
and on your way at last,
the rings of Saturn brilliant
as pain, your dark craft
nosing its way through stars.
You've been gone now
how many years?

Hot metal hurtles over your eyes,
razors the flesh, recedes;
this is the universe
too, this burnt view.

Deepfreeze in blankets; tubes feed you,
your hurt cells glow & tick;
when the time comes you will wake
naked and mended, on earth again, to find
the rest of us changed and older.

Meanwhile your body
hums you to sleep, you cruise
among the nebulae, ice glass
on the bedside table,
the shining pitcher, your white cloth feet
which blaze with reflected light
against the harsh black shadow
behind the door.

Hush, say the hands
of the nurses, drawing the blinds
down   hush
says your drifting blood,
cool stardust.

BLUE DWARFS

Tree burial, you tell me, that's
the way. Not up in but under.
Rootlets & insects, you say as we careen
along the highway with the news on
through a wind thickening with hayfever.
Last time it was fire.

It's a problem, what to do
with yourself after you're dead.
Then there's before.

The scabby wild plums fall from the tree
as I climb it, branches & leaves
peeling off under my bootsoles.
They vanish into the bone-coloured
grass & mauve asters
or lie among the rocks and the stench
of woodchucks, bursting & puckered
and oozing juice & sweet pits & yellow
pulp but still
burning, cool and blue
as the cores of the old stars
that shrivel out there in multiples
of zero. Pinpoint mouths
burrowing in them. I pick up the good ones
which won't last long either.

If there's a tree for you it should be
this one. Here
it is, your six-quart basket
of blue light, sticky
and fading but more than
still edible. Time smears
our hands all right, we lick it off, a windfall.

HIGH SUMMER

High summer,
our lives here winding down.

Why are we building fences?
There's nothing we can keep out.

Wild mustard, hornworms, cutworms
push at the edges of this space

it's taken eight years to clear.
The fields, lush green and desolate

as promises, are still pretending
to be owned. Nothing

is owned, not even the graves
across the road with the names

so squarely marked.
Goodbye, we credit

the apple trees, dead
and alive, with saying.

They say no such thing.

LAST DAY

This is the last day of the last week.
It's June, the evenings touching
our skins like plush, milkweeds sweetening
the sticky air which pulses
with moths, their powdery wings and velvet
tongues. In the dusk, nighthawks and the fluting
voices from the pond, its edges
webbed with spawn. Everything
leans into the pulpy moon.

In the mornings the hens
make egg after egg, warty-shelled
and perfect; the henhouse floor
packed with old shit and winter straw
trembles with flies, green and silver.

Who wants to leave it, who wants it
to end, water moving
against water, skin
against skin? We wade
through moist sun-
light towards nothing, which is oval

and full. This egg
in my hand is our last meal,
you break it open and the sky
turns orange again and the sun rises
again and this is the last day again.

From
MURDER IN THE DARK
1983

BREAD

Imagine a piece of bread. You don't have to imagine it, it's right here in the kitchen, on the bread board, in its plastic bag, lying beside the bread knife. The bread knife is an old one you picked up at an auction; it has the word BREAD carved into the wooden handle. You open the bag, pull back the wrapper, cut yourself a slice. You put butter on it, then peanut butter, then honey, and you fold it over. Some of the honey runs out onto your fingers and you lick it off. It takes you about a minute to eat the bread. This bread happens to be brown, but there is also white bread, in the refrigerator, and a heel of rye you got last week, round as a full stomach then, now going mouldy. Occasionally you make bread. You think of it as something relaxing to do with your hands.

*

Imagine a famine. Now imagine a piece of bread. Both of these things are real but you happen to be in the same room with only one of them. Put yourself into a different room, that's what the mind is for. You are now lying on a thin mattress in a hot room. The walls are made of dried earth and your sister, who is younger than you are, is in the room with you. She is starving, her belly is bloated, flies land on her eyes; you brush them off with your hand. You have a cloth too, filthy but damp, and you press it to her lips and forehead. The piece of bread is the bread you've been saving, for days it seems. You are as hungry as she is, but not yet as weak. How long does this take? When will someone come with more bread? You think of going out to see if you might find something that could be eaten, but outside the streets are infested with scavengers and the stink of corpses is everywhere.

Should you share the bread or give the whole piece to your sister? Should you eat the piece of bread yourself? After all, you have a better chance of living, you're stronger. How long does it take to decide?

*

Imagine a prison. There is something you know that you have not yet told. Those in control of the prison know that you know.

94

So do those not in control. If you tell, thirty or forty or a hundred of your friends, your comrades, will be caught and will die. If you refuse to tell, tonight will be like last night. They always choose the night. You don't think about the night however, but about the piece of bread they offered you. How long does it take? The piece of bread was brown and fresh and reminded you of sunlight falling across a wooden floor. It reminded you of a bowl, a yellow bowl that was once in your home. It held apples and pears; it stood on a table you can also remember. It's not the hunger or the pain that is killing you but the absence of the yellow bowl. If you could only hold the bowl in your hands, right here, you could withstand anything, you tell yourself. The bread they offered you is subversive, it's treacherous, it does not mean life.

*

There were once two sisters. One was rich and had no children, the other had five children and was a widow, so poor that she no longer had any food left. She went to her sister and asked her for a mouthful of bread. 'My children are dying,' she said. The rich sister said, 'I do not have enough for myself,' and drove her away from the door. Then the husband of the rich sister came home and wanted to cut himself a piece of bread; but when he made the first cut, out flowed red blood.

Everyone knew what that meant.

This is a traditional German fairy-tale.

*

The loaf of bread I have conjured for you floats about a foot above your kitchen table. The table is normal, there are no trap doors in it. A blue tea towel floats beneath the bread, and there are no strings attaching the cloth to the bread or the bread to the ceiling or the table to the cloth, you've proved it by passing your hand above and below. You didn't touch the bread though. What stopped you? You don't want to know whether the bread is real or whether it's just a hallucination I've somehow duped you into seeing. There's no doubt that you can see the bread, you can even smell it, it smells like yeast, and it looks solid enough, solid as your own arm. But can you trust it? Can you eat it? You don't want to know, imagine that.

THE PAGE

1. The page waits, pretending to be blank. Is that its appeal, its blankness? What else is this smooth and white, this terrifyingly innocent? A snowfall, a glacier? It's a desert, totally arid, without life. But people venture into such places. Why? To see how much they can endure, how much dry light?

2. I've said the page is white, and it is: white as wedding dresses, rare whales, seagulls, angels, ice and death. Some say that like sunlight it contains all colours; others, that it's white because it's hot, it will burn out your optic nerves; that those who stare at the page too long go blind.

3. The page itself has no dimensions and no directions. There's no up or down except what you yourself mark, there's no thickness and weight but those you put there, north and south do not exist unless you're certain of them. The page is without vistas and without sounds, without centres or edges. Because of this you can become lost in it forever. Have you never seen the look of gratitude, the look of joy, on the faces of those who have managed to return from the page? Despite their faintness, their loss of blood, they fall on their knees, they push their hands into the earth, they clasp the bodies of those they love, or, in a pinch, any bodies they can get, with an urgency unknown to those who have never experienced the full horror of a journey into the page.

4. If you decide to enter the page, take a knife and some matches, and something that will float. Take something you can hold onto, and a prism to split the light and a talisman that works, which should be hung on a chain around your neck: that's for getting back. It doesn't matter what kind of shoes, but your hands should be bare. You should never go into the page with gloves on. Such decisions, needless to say, should not be made lightly.

   There are those, of course, who enter the page without deciding, without meaning to. Some of these have charmed lives and no difficulty, but most never make it out at all. For them the page appears as well, a lovely pool in which they catch sight of a face, their own but better. These unfortunates do not jump: rather they fall, and the page closes over their heads without a sound, without a seam, and is immediately as whole and empty, as glassy, as enticing as before.

5. The question about the page is: what is beneath it? It seems to have only two dimensions, you can pick it up and turn it over and the back is the same as the front. Nothing, you say, disappointed.

But you were looking in the wrong place, you were looking *on the back* instead of *beneath*. *Beneath the page* is another story. Beneath the page is a story. Beneath the page is everything that has ever happened, most of which you would rather not hear about.

The page is not a pool but a skin, a skin is there to hold in and it can feel you touching it. Did you really think it would just lie there and do nothing?

Touch the page at your peril: it is you who are blank and innocent, not the page. Nevertheless you want to know, nothing will stop you. You touch the page, it's as if you've drawn a knife across it, the page has been hurt now, a sinuous wound opens, a thin incision. Darkness wells through.

MUTE

Whether to speak or not: the question that comes up again when you think you've said too much, again. Another clutch of nouns, a fistful: look how they pick them over, the shoppers for words, pinching here and there to see if they're bruised yet. Verbs are no better, they wind them up, let them go, scrabbling over the table, wind them up again too tight and the spring breaks. You can't take another poem of spring, not with the wound-up vowels, not with the bruised word green in it, not yours, not with ants crawling all over it, not this infestation. It's a market, flyspecked; how do you wash a language? There's the beginning of a bad smell, you can hear the growls, something's being eaten, once too often. Your mouth feels rotted.

Why involve yourself? You'd do better to sit off to the side, on the sidewalk under the awning, hands over your mouth, your ears, your eyes, with a cup in front of you into which people will or will not drop pennies. They think you can't talk, they're sorry for you, but. But you're waiting for the word, the one that will finally be right. A compound, the generation of life, mud and light.

SHE

knows exactly what she's doing. Well, why not? Along the
street, around the corner, the piece of her that's just disap-
pearing. If that's the way it works, that's what she'll do. Some-
times in shorts, with tanned thighs, or with sleeves like cab-
bages, or the whole body falling liquid from the shoulders:
whatever's about to happen. Lace at the throat, the ankle,
skimming the breasts, wherever they're putting it this year,
and a laugh or not, at the pulsepoint. What will it get her?
Something. You have to know when to run and where, how to
close a door, gently. Just a little showing, something that looks
like flesh, they follow, a few white stones dropped in the forest,
under the trees, shining in the moonlight, clues, a trail. To get
from one point to the next and then see another, and another
beyond that. She deals in longing, the sickness of the heart,
stuttering of the arteries, would you call it suffering, where
does it lead? Deeper into the forest, deeper into the moonlight.
They think they'll come out from among the trees and she will
be there, finally waiting, for them, all cool white light.

WORSHIP

You have these sores in your mouth that will not heal. It's from
eating too much sugar, you tell yourself. To the gods men offer
flowers and food, remember those chrysanthemums, those
pumpkins, at the altar, even in that square brick church? The
one that smelled like wet feet, wearing socks, for a long time.
Thanksgiving. That's why he brings you roses, on occasion,
and chocolates when he can't think of anything else. For the
same reasons too: worship or ritual or sucking up. Prayer is
wanting. Jesus, Jesus he says, but he's not praying to Jesus,
he's praying to you, not to your body or your face but to that
space you hold at the centre, which is the shape of the universe.
Empty. He wants response, an answer from that dark sphere
and its red stars, which he can touch but not see. How does it
feel to be a god, for five minutes anyway? Now you know what

they have to put up with. Those groans that sound so much like suffering and perhaps are, you can't tell by listening.

You aren't really a god but despite that you are silent. When you're being worshipped there isn't much to say. It's White Gift Sunday, tinned goods this time, in tissue paper, for the poor, and that's you up there, shining, burning, like a candle, like a chalice, burnished; with use and service. After you've been serviced, after you've been used, you'll be put away again until needed.

ICONOGRAPHY

He wants her arranged just so. He wants her, arranged. He arranges to want her.

This is the arrangement they have made. With strings attached, or ropes, stockings, leather straps. What else is arranged? Furniture, flowers. For contemplation and a graceful disposition of parts to compose a unified and aesthetic whole.

Once she wasn't supposed to like it. To have her in a position she didn't like, that was power. Even if she liked it she had to pretend she didn't. Then she was supposed to like it. To make her do something she didn't like and then make her like it, that was greater power. The greatest power of all is when she doesn't really like it but she's supposed to like it, so she has to pretend.

Whether he's making her like it or making her dislike it or making her pretend to like it is important but it's not the most important thing. The most important thing is making her. Over, from nothing, new. From scratch, the way he wants.

It can never be known whether she likes it or not. By this time she doesn't know herself. All you see is the skin, that smile of hers, flat but indelible, like a tattoo. Hard to tell, and she never will, she can't. They don't get into it unless they like it, he says. He has the last word. He has the word.

Watch yourself. That's what the mirrors are for, this story is a mirror story which rhymes with horror story, almost but not quite. We fall back into these rhythms as if into safe hands.

STRAWBERRIES

The strawberries when I first remember them are not red but blue, that blue flare, before the whitehot part of the wire, sun glancing from the points of waves. It was the heat that made things blue like that, rage, I went into the waste orchard because I did not want to talk to you or even see you, I wanted instead to do something small and useful that I was good at. It was June, there were mosquitoes, I stirred them up as I pushed aside the higher stems, but I didn't care, I was immune, all that adrenalin kept them away, and if not I was in the mood for minor lacerations. I don't get angry like that any more. I almost miss it.

I'd like to say I saw everything through a haze of red; which is not true. Nothing was hazy. Everything was very clear, clearer than usual, my hands with the stained nails, the sunlight falling on the ground through the apple-tree branches, each leaf, each white five petalled yellow centred flower and conical fine-haired dark red multi-seeded dwarf berry rendering itself in dry flat two dimensional detail, like background foliage by one of the crazier Victorian painters, just before the invention of the camera; and at some time during that hour, though not for the whole hour, I forgot what things were called and saw instead what they are.

HIM

Every time, when you open the door to him, it's much the same: as if he's just come from another planet, he stands there semi-blinded, by the sudden light, as if you are shedding it, from within, as if he is his own dark hurtling gravity-free interior and he's just landed and you are the land. He knows he has to make his alien greeting and you know it too, it will be courteous, and awkward because of his difficulties with the language. *I come in peace*, you want to prompt him, but don't. He's anxious enough already. It's the way he inclines his head, looking instead at the floor, having looked at you first with eyes so unprotected and candid you couldn't look back. Like many other sad men, he wants only to be allowed. To be taken in.

You're tired of the sadnesss of men, it's been used on you too often, sadness like a clumsy plumber's wrench, a tool for bludgeoning water. Sadness has been offered as a good reason for you to do all sorts of things. He's not offering it. He's not without sadness but he's no purveyor of his own grief, he's unconscious of it; he's unconscious. He likes watching well-played games.

You want to get fancy, you want to say, he's like a tree or a stone, one of those mute contained objects, but for once you avoid metaphors: there's nothing else you want to change him into. Your years of practice, that skill in metamorphosis, count for nothing here. How many times have you awakened in the moonlight and seen those indigo shadows instead of eyes, hard as if cast by granite, and thought, I'm in bed with a killer? You can crumple all that time up with one hand now and throw it away.

Your worst fear is that you might have missed this. Still, you have to come clean and it angers you; but how can it? Isn't this what you wanted? Isn't this the man through whom all men can be forgiven? Must be forgiven, because now you're beginning to remember the way the others were partly like him.

HOPELESS

Today I seem to myself merely sentimental, at the window, looking out at the slush and worrying about the Book of Job. Religion, the burnt heart gripped in its ritual thorns, the chest wall open like a display window. Why are there hookworms? Why are there explosions, on the road, in the wrists, blood hazing the ionosphere?

Forget about tough and competent, I can pour boiling lead from the battlements with one hand, I'm used to it by now, I hardly even look at the scorched faces down there, open mouths with their needle-pointed weasel teeth and all those enraged flags waving around. That's what I do on weekdays, during invasions, but today is Sunday and I'm hopeless, we're hopeless. Hope needs the future tense, which only makes you greedy and a hoarder: the future is what you save up for but like thunder it's only an echo, a reverse dream. Hope is when you expect something more, and what more is there?

Outside, the plague bulges, slops over, flows down the streets and so we stay here, holding on and holding on, to the one small thing which is not yet withering, not yet marked for death, this armful of words, *together*, *with*. This is as good as it gets, nothing can be better and so there's nothing to hope for, but I do it anyway. In the distance, beyond the war in the midground, there's a river, and some willows, in sunlight, and some hills.

A PARABLE

I'm in a room with no windows that open and no doors that close, which may sound like an insane asylum but is actually only a room, the room where I'm sitting to write to you once more, one more letter, one more piece of paper, deaf, dumb and blind. When I'm finished I will throw it into the air and as we say it will disappear, but the air will not think so.

I'm listening to your questions. The reason I don't answer them is that they are not questions at all. Is there any answer to a stone or the sun? *What is this for?* you say, to which the only possible reply is that we are not all utilitarians. *Who are you really* is the question asked by the worm of the apple on the way through. A gnawed core may be the centre but is it the reality?

As for me, I may not be anything at all but the space between your right hand and your left hand when your hands are on my shoulders. I keep your right hand and your left hand apart, through me they also touch. It feels like silence, which is a sound also. I am the time it takes you to think about that. You enter my time, you leave it, I cannot enter or leave, why ask me? You know what it looks like and I don't. Mirrors are no use at all.

Ask me instead who you are: when you walk into this room through the door that isn't there, it's not myself I see but you.

HAND

Your body lies on the floor, with or without you. Your eyes are closed. No good to say you are your body, though this also is true, because at the moment you are not; you are only a fist tightening somewhere at the back of the neck. It's this fist that holds you clenched and pushes you forward with short jabs of pain, it's this fist that drives you through time, along those windowless corridors we know so well, where the yellowish-white light sucks the blood from the surface of your face and your feet in their narrowing shoes hit cement, a thud and then another, clockwork. This fist is what I must open: to let you in.

I begin with the back of the neck, lightly, feeling the involved knot of muscle, in its own grip, a puzzle. A false start, to press too hard here would bruise you. I move to the feet and begin again.

The feet must be taught to see in the dark, because the dark is where they walk. The feet learn quietly; they are wiser than the eyes, they are hard to fool, like stones they are heavy and grave, they desire nothing for themselves, once they have seen they remember. I move my thumbs down between the tendons, push on the deaf white soles of the imprisoned feet.

This is your body I hold between both of my hands, its eyes closed. Now your body has become a hand that is opening, your body is the hand of a blind man, reaching out into a darkness which may in fact be light; for all you know. Behind your closed eyes the filaments of a tree unwind, take shape, red and purple, blue, a slow glow. This is not a lovers' scenario. This is the journey of the body, its hesitant footsteps as it walks back into its own flesh. I close my own eyes so I can see better where we are going. My hands move forward by knowledge and guess; my hands move you forward. Your eyes are closed but the third eye, the eye of the body, is opening. It floats before you like a ring of blue fire. Now you see into it and through it.

EVERLASTING

I reach down and what do I come up with? Something early, a small dry white flower. Everlasting, it was called. Picked by the roadside, highway, near a rockface shot through with quartz; on which the sun shone as it rose, lighting up the rock like glass, like an entrance into light. Right then the world was something you could walk through, into.

You could tent then, anywhere, just beside the road, any wide place. The tents were heavy canvas and smelled of tar. The others put the fire out. There were almost no cars; it was because of the war. The war was happening somewhere, and the devil's paintbrushes, red and orange, grew there in clumps, purple vetch, daisies with their heavy smell, tiny black ants on the petals. A stream too, the water brownish and clear.

There was nothing to do, there was all that time, which did not need to be filled. I knelt down, bare skin on the damp ground, and reached into the absence of time and came up with a handful of stems, on their ends the light reflecting from the stream, the dry white flowers, already eternal.

INSTRUCTIONS FOR THE THIRD EYE

The eye is the organ of vision, and the third eye is no exception to that. Open it and it sees, close it and it doesn't.

Most people have a third eye but they don't trust it. That wasn't really F., standing on the corner, hands in his overcoat pocket, waiting for the light to change: F. died two months ago. It's a trick my eyes played on me, they say. A trick of the light.

I've got nothing against telepathy, said Jane; but the telephone is so much more dependable.

*

What's the difference between vision and a vision? The former relates to something it's assumed you've seen, the latter to something it's assumed you haven't. Language is not always dependable either.

*

If you want to use the third eye you must close the other two. Then breathe evenly; then wait. This sometimes works; on the other hand, sometimes you merely go to sleep. That sometimes works also.

*

When you've had enough practice you don't have to bother with these preliminary steps. You find too that what you see depends partly on what you want to look at and partly on how. As I said, the third eye is only an eye.

*

There are some who resent the third eye. They would have it removed, if they could. They feel it as a parasite, squatting in the centre of the forehead, feeding on the brain.

To them the third eye shows only the worst scenery: the gassed and scorched corpses at the cave-mouth, the gutted babies, the spoor left by generals, and, closer to home, the hearts gone bubonic with jealousy and greed, glinting through the vests and sweaters of anyone at all. Torment, they say and see. The third eye can be merciless, especially when wounded.

*

But someone has to see these things. They exist. Try not to resist the third eye: it knows what it's doing. Leave it alone and it will show you that this truth is not the only truth. One day you will wake up and everything, the stones by the driveway, the brick houses, each brick, each leaf of each tree, your own body, will be glowing from within, lit up, so bright you can hardly look. You will reach out in any direction and you will touch the light itself.

*

After that there are no more instructions because there is no more choice. You see. You see.

From
INTERLUNAR
1984

Snake Poems

SNAKE WOMAN

I was once the snake woman,

the only person, it seems, in the whole place
who wasn't terrified of them.

I used to hunt with two sticks
among milkweed and under porches and logs
for this vein of cool green metal
which would run through my fingers like mercury
or turn to a raw bracelet
gripping my wrist:

I could follow them by their odour,
a sick smell, acid and glandular,
part skunk, part inside
of a torn stomach,
the smell of their fear.

Once caught, I'd carry them,
limp and terrorized, into the dining room,
something even men were afraid of.
What fun I had!
Put that thing in my bed and I'll kill you.

Now, I don't know.
Now I'd consider the snake.

LESSON ON SNAKES

Pinned down, this one
opens it mouth as wide as it can
showing fangs and a throat
like the view down a pink lily,
double tongue curved out like stamens.

The lilies do it to keep
from being eaten, this dance of snakes

and the snakes do it to keep from being
eaten also. Since they cannot talk:

the snake is a mute
except for the sound like steam
escaping from a radiator
it makes when cornered:
something punctured and leaking.

This one is green and yellow,
striped like a moose maple.
Sweetly and with grace it hunts
a glimpse, a rustle
among the furry strawberries.

It's hardly
the devil in your garden
but a handy antidote to mice

and yet you'd batter it
with that hoe or crowbar
to a twist of slack rope:

a bad answer
to anything that gets in
what you think is your way.

LIES ABOUT SNAKES

I present the glass snake
which is supposed to break when stepped on
but doesn't. One more lie about snakes,

nor is it transparent. Nothing
could be more opaque. Watch it
there as it undulates over the sand,
a movement of hips in a tight skirt.
You remember the legends
of snakes which were changed to women
and vice versa. Another lie.

Other lies about snakes:
that they cause thunder,
that they won't cross ropes,
that they travel in pairs:
(even when together
for warmth at night or in winter,
snakes are alone)

Swaying up from coiled baskets
they move as if to music,
but snakes cannot hear music.
The time they keep is their own.

BAD MOUTH

There are no leaf-eating snakes.
All are fanged and gorge on blood.
Each one is a hunter's hunter,
nothing more than an endless gullet
pulling itself on over the still-alive prey
like a sock gone ravenous, like an evil glove,
like sheer greed, lithe and devious.

Puff adder buried in hot sand
or poisoning the toes of boots,
for whom killing is easy and careless
as war, as digestion,
why should you be spared?

And you, *Constrictor constrictor*,
sinuous ribbon of true darkness,
one long muscle with eyes and an anus,
looping like thick tar out of the trees
to squeeze the voice from anything edible,
reducing it to scales and belly.

And you, pit viper
with your venomous pallid throat
and teeth like syringes
and your nasty radar
homing in on the deep red shadow
nothing else knows it casts . . .
Shall I concede these deaths?

Between us there is no fellow feeling,
as witness: a snake cannot scream.
Observe the alien
chainmail skin, straight out
of science fiction, pure
shiver, pure saturn.

Those who can explain them
can explain anything.

Some say they're a snarled puzzle
only gasoline and a match can untangle.
Even their mating is barely sexual,
a romance between two lengths
a cyanide-coloured string.
Despite their live births and squirming nests
it's hard to believe in snakes loving.

Alone among the animals
the snake does not sing.
The reason for them is the same
as the reason for stars, and not human.

EATING SNAKE

I too have taken the god into my mouth,
chewed it up and tried not to choke on the bones.
Rattlesnake it was, panfried
and good too though a little oily.

(Forget the phallic symbolism:
two differences:
snake tastes like chicken,
and who ever credited the prick with wisdom?)

All peoples are driven
to the point of eating their gods
after a time: it's the old greed
for a plateful of outer space, that craving for darkness,
the lust to feel what it does to you
when your teeth meet in divinity, in the flesh,
when you swallow it down
and you can see with its own cold eyes,
look out through murder.

This is a lot of fuss to make about mere lunch:
metaphysics with onions.
The snake was not served with its tail in its mouth
as would have been appropriate.
Instead the cook nailed the skin to the wall,
complete with rattles, and the head was mounted.
It was only a snake after all.

(Nevertheless, the authorities are agreed:
God is round.)

METEMPSYCHOSIS

Somebody's grandmother glides through the bracken,
in widow's black and graceful
and sharp as ever: see how her eyes glitter!

Who were you when you were a snake?

This one was a dancer who is now
a green streamer waved by its own breeze
and here's your blunt striped uncle, come back
to bask under the wicker chairs
on the porch and watch over you.

Unfurling itself from its cast skin,
the snake proclaims resurrection
to all believers

though some tire soon of being born
over and over; for them there's the breath
that shivers in the yellow grass,
a papery finger, half of a noose, a summons
to the dead river.

Who's that in the cold cellar
with the apples and the rats? Whose is
that voice of a husk rasping in the wind?
Your lost child whispering *Mother*,
the one more child you never had,
you child who wants back in.

THE WHITE SNAKE

The white snake is to be found, says legend,
at the dark of the moon,
by the forks of roads, under three-leaved trees,
at the bottoms of unsounded lakes.

It looks like water
freezing. It has no eyes.
It lays quartz eggs and foretells the future.

If you can find it and eat it
then you will understand
the languages of the animals.

There was a man who tried it.
He hunted, caught, transformed
the sacred body of living snow
into raw meat, cut into it, swallowed.

Then sound poured over him
like a wall breaking, like a disaster:

He went blind in an instant.
Light rose in him
filling his mouth like blood,
like earth in the mouth of a man buried.

Human speech left him.
For the rest of his life, emptied and mute
he could do nothing but listen
to the words, words around him everywhere like rain falling.

Beware of the white snake, says the story.
Choose ignorance.

(There are no white snakes in nature.)

PSALM TO SNAKE

O snake, you are an argument
for poetry:

a shift among dry leaves
when there is no wind,
a thin line moving through

that which is not
time, creating time,
a voice from the dead, oblique

and silent. A movement
from left to right,
a vanishing. Prophet under a stone.

I know you're there
even when I can't see you

I see the trail you make
in the blank sand, in the morning

I see the point
of intersection, the whiplash
across the eye. I see the kill.

O long word, cold-blooded and perfect

QUATTROCENTO

The snake enters your dreams through paintings:
this one, of a formal garden
in which there are always three:

the thin man with the green-white skin
that marks him vegetarian
and the woman with a swayback and hard breasts
that look stuck on

and the snake, vertical and with a head
that's face-coloured and haired like a woman's.

Everyone looks unhappy,
even the few zoo animals, stippled with sun,
even the angel who's like a slab
of flaming laundry, hovering
up there with his sword of fire,
unable as yet to strike.

There's no love here.
Maybe it's the boredom.

And that's no apple but a heart
torn out of someone
in this myth gone suddenly Aztec.

This is the possibility of death
the snake is offering:
death upon death squeezed together,
a blood snowball.

To devour it is to fall out
of the still unending noon
to a hard ground with a straight horizon

and you are no longer the
idea of a body but a body,
you slide down into your body as into hot mud.

You feel the membranes of disease
close over your head, and history
occurs to you and space enfolds

you in its armies, in its nights, and you
must learn to see in darkness.

Here you can praise the light,
having so little of it:

it's the death you carry in you
red and captured, that makes the world
shine for you
as it never did before.

This is how you learn prayer.

Love is choosing, the snake said.
The kingdom of god is within you
because you ate it.

AFTER HERACLITUS

The snake is one name of God,
my teacher said:
All nature is a fire
we burn in and are
renewed, one skin
shed and then another.

To talk with the body
is what the snake does, letter
after letter formed on the grass,
itself a tongue, looping its earthy hieroglyphs,
the sunlight praising it
as it shines there on the doorstep,
a green light blessing your house.

This is the voice
you could pray to for the answers
to your sickness:
leave it a bowl of milk,
watch it drink

You do not pray, but go for the shovel,
old blood on the blade

But pick it up and you would hold
the darkness that you fear
turned flesh and embers,
cool power coiling into your wrists
and it would be in your hands
where it always has been.

This is the nameless one
giving itself a name,
one among many

and your own name as well.

You know this and still kill it.

THE BLUE SNAKE

The snake winds through your head
into the temple which stands on a hill
and is not much visited now.

Toppled stones clutter the paving
where the blue snake swims towards you,
dry in the dry air
blue as a vein or a fading bruise.
It looks at you from the side of its head
as snakes do. It flickers.

What does it know
that it needs to tell you?
What do you need to be told?

You are surprised to hear it speak.
It has the voice of a flute
when you first blow into it,
long and breathless; it has an old voice,

like the blue stars, like the unborn,
the voice of things beginning and ceasing.

As you listen, you grow heavier.
It asks you why you are here,
and you can't answer.

It begins to glow,
it's almost transparent now,
you can see the spine
with its many pairs of delicate ribs
unrolling like a feather.

This has gone far enough,
you think, and turn away.
It isn't what you came for.

Behind you the snakes dissolves
and flows into the rock.

On the plain below you is a river
you know you must follow home.

Interlunar

DOORWAY

I seem to myself to be without power.
To have the power of waiting merely.
Waiting to be told what to say.
But who will tell me?

November is the month of entrance,
month of descent. Which has passed easily,
which has been lenient with me this year.
Nobody's blood on the floor.

My arm lies across this oak desk
in the fading sunlight of four o'clock,
the skin warming, alive still,
the hand unspoken.

Through the window
below the half-lowered blind, there are
the herbs frost-killed in their boxes,
life retreating to the roots;
beyond them, the rubbishy laneway
owned by nobody.
Where all power is either spent or potential.

Power of the grey stone
resting inert, not shaping itself.
Power of the murdered girl's
bone in the stream, not yet a flute.
Power of a door unopened.

BEFORE

For John T.

A bowl of cooked earth, holding
itself in another form:
the last apples of this winter,
wizened and sticky.
Possibly not food.

Even the weak spring sunlight
waning through the four small panes
is excess for him:
his eyes slit against it.

A knife, left over from last night,
eases to the surface, turns over
lazily, floats there,
a fish rising
in brown swamp water,
silver and dead.

Some woman or other,
damp handfuls of flesh
and no questions.
He is fat bait.

Desire gathers
icy and glistening, along
the buds of the forsythia
about to open.

Who cares who cares.
He would rather be a black stone
in the dirt back of the garden
or God. The same thing.

The hoe and the mattock lean in the corner.

Out there,
along the edge of the saltmarsh
two crows level, their wings
radiating darkness.

It's only one version.
So is the sun.

BEDSIDE

You sit beside the bed
in the *extremis* ward, holding your father's feet
as you have not done since you were a child.
You would hold his hands, but they are strapped down,
emptied at last of power.

He can see, possibly, the weave of the sheet
that covers him from chest to ankles;
he does not wish to.

He has been opened. He is at the mercy.

You hold his feet,
not moving. You would like
to drag him back. You remember
how you have judged each other
in silence, relentlessly.

You listen intently, as if for a signal,
to the undersea ping of the monitors,
the waterlogged lungs breathed into by machines,
the heart, wired for sound
and running too quickly in the stuck body,

the murderous body, the body
itself stalled in a field of ice
that spreads out endlessly under it,
the snowdrifts tucked by the wind around
the limbs and torso.

Now he is walking
somewhere you cannot follow,
leaving no footprints.
Already in this whiteness
he casts no shadow.

THE SAINTS

The saints cannot distinguish
between being with other people and being
alone: another good reason for becoming one.

They live in trees and eat air.
Staring past or through us, they see
things which we would call not there.
We on the contrary see them.

They smell of old fur coats
stored for a long time in the attic.
When they move they ripple.
Two of them passed here yesterday,
filled and vacated and filled
by the wind, like drained pillows
blowing across a derelict lot,
their twisted and scorched feet
not touching the ground,
their feathers catching in thistles.
What they touched emptied of colour.

Whether they are dead or not
is a moot point.
Shreds of them litter history,
a hand here, a bone there:
is it suffering or goodness
that makes them holy,
or can anyone tell the difference?

Though they pray, they do not pray
for us. Prayers peel off them
like burned skin healing.
Once they tried to save something,
others or their own souls.
Now they seem to have no use,
like the colours on blind fish.
Nevertheless they are sacred.

They drift through the atmosphere,
their blue eyes sucked dry
by the ordeal of seeing,
exuding gaps in the landscape as water
exudes mist. They blink
and reality shivers.

NOMADS

A woman speaking of a man
thinking she means comfort
when what in fact she means is
blood in the bathtub.
Or it could be a man speaking
about a woman.

The nomads file past us
in the forests
at night, their eyes picking up
the minor light, like an owl's,
going their rounds. Going
home, which is motion.
The children sleeping on the warm backs
among the fur and hair.
The craving for arms around
us; the belief we need
that the trees love us.

He's so good, she says,
knowing already the hole *No* makes
in the center of her forehead
where the eye was once that could
see it coming.
The outline of him stands
over there, against
the wall, devoid of features.
She should know by now
the disguises your own death takes
when it really wants you.

PRECOGNITION

Living backwards means only
I must suffer everything twice.
Those picnics were already loss:
with the dragonflies and the clear streams halfway.

What good did it do me to know
how far along you would come with me
and when you would return?
By yourself, to a life you call daily.

You did not consider me a soul
but a landscape, not even one
I recognize as mine, but foreign
and rich in curios:
an egg of blue marble,
a dried pod,
a clay goddess you picked up at a stall
somewhere among the dun and dust-green
hills and the bronze-hot
sun and the odd shadows,

not knowing what would be protection,
or even the need for it then.

I wake in the early dawn and there is the roadway
shattered, and the glass and blood,
from an intersection that has happened
already, though I can't say when.
Simply that it will happen.

What could I tell you now that would keep you
safe or warn you?
What good would it do?
Live and be happy.

I would rather cut myself loose
from time, shave off my hair
and stand at a crossroads
with a wooden bowl, throwing
myself on the dubious mercy
of the present, which is innocent
and forgetful and hits the eye bare

and without words and without even love
than do this mourning over.

KEEP

I know that you will die
before I do.

Already your skin tastes faintly
of the acid that is eating through you.

None of this, none of this is true,
no more than a leaf is botany,

along this avenue of old maples
the birds fall down through the branches
as the long slow rain of small bodies
falls like snow through the darkening sea,

wet things in turn move up out of the earth,
your body is liquid in my hands, almost
a piece of solid water.

Time is what we're doing,
I'm falling into the flesh,
into the sadness of the body
that cannot give up its habits,
habits of the hands and skin.

I will be one of those old women
with good bones and stringy necks
who will not let go of anything.

You'll be there. You'll keep
your distance,
the same one.

ANCHORAGE

This is the sea then, once
again, warm this time
and swarming. Sores fester
on your feet in the tepid

beach water, where French
wine bottles float among grape-
fruit peels and the stench of death
from the piles of sucked-out shells
and emptied lunches.
Here is a pool with nurse sharks
kept for the tourists
and sea turtles scummy with algae,
winging their way through their closed
heaven of dirty stones. Here
is where the good ship *Envious*
rides at anchor.
The land is red with hibiscus
and smells of piss; and here
beside the houses built on stilts,
warped in the salt and heat,
they plant their fathers in the yards,
cover them with cement
tender as blankets:

Drowned at sea, the same one
the mermaids swim in, hairy
and pallid, with rum on the beach after.
But that's a day trip.
Further along, there are tents
where the fishers camp,
cooking their stews of claws
and spines, and at dawn they steer
further out than you'd think
possible, between the killer
water and the killer sun,
carried on hollow pieces
of wood with the names of women,
not sweethearts
only but mothers, clumsy
and matronly, though their ribbed bodies
are fragile as real bodies
and like them also a memory,
and like them also two hands
held open, and like them also
the last hope of safety.

A SUNDAY DRIVE

The skin seethes in the heat
which roars out from the sun, wave after tidal wave;
the sea is flat and hot and too bright,
stagnant as a puddle,
edged by a beach reeking of shit.
The city is like a city
bombed out and burning;
the smell of smoke is everywhere,
drifting from the mounds of rubble.
Now and then a new tower,
already stained, lifts from the tangle;
the cars stall and bellow.
From the trampled earth rubbish erupts
and huts of tin and warped boards
and cloth and anything scavenged.
Everything is the colour of dirt
except the kites, red and purple,
three of them, fluttering cheerfully
from a slope of garbage,
and the womens' dresses, cleaned somehow,
vaporous and brilliant, and the dutiful
white smiles of the child beggars
who kiss your small change
and press it to their heads and hearts.

Uncle, they call you. Mother.
I have never felt less motherly.
The moon is responsible for all this,
goddess of increase
and death, which here are the same.
Why try to redeem
anything? In this maze
of condemned flesh without beginning or end
where the pulp of the body steams and bloats
and spawns and multiplies itself
the wise man chooses serenity.

Here you are taught the need to be holy,
to wash a lot and live apart.
Burial by fire is the last mercy:
decay is reserved for the living.

The desire to be loved is the last illusion:
Give it up and you will be free.

Bombay, 1982

II

ONE SPECIES OF LOVE,
AFTER A PAINTING
BY HIERONYMOUS BOSCH

In the foreground there are a lot of stones,
each one painted singly
and in detail.

There is a man, sitting down.
Behind the man is a hill,
shaped like a mound burial
or a pudding,
with scrubby bushes, the leaves glazed
by the serene eye-colour of the sky.
In the middle distance, an invisible line
beyond which things become
abruptly bluer.

At the man's feet there is a lion,
plush-furred and blunted,
and in the right foreground, a creature
part bird, part teapot,
part lizard and part hat
is coming out of an eggshell.

The man himself, in his robe
the muted pink of the ends of fingers
is gazing up at the half-sized
woman who is suspended
in the air over his head.

She has wings, but they aren't moving.
She's blue, like the background,
denoting holiness or distance
or perhaps lack of a body.

She holds one hand in a gesture
of benediction which is a little wooden.
The other hand points to the ground.

There is no sound in this picture,
light but no shadows.
The stones keep still.
The surface is clear
and without texture.

GISELLE IN DAYTIME

You know the landscape: in the distance
three low hills, bare of snow.

In the foreground the willow grove
along the unmoving river
not icebound. Snow in the shadows though.
A diffused light that is not the sun.

Here and there, the young girls
in their white dresses made of paper
not written on.
No one is here willingly.
None are mourners.

Each stays under a separate tree,
sitting or standing as if
aimless. It was not
an end they wanted but more life.

The near one crouches on the chilled
sand, knees to belly,
holding in her hands a plain stone
she turns over and over,

puzzled, searching for the cut in it
where the blood ran out.

The tree arching above her
is dead, like everything
here. Nevertheless it sways, although there is
no wind, quickening and shaking out
for her its thin leaves and small green flowers,

which has never happened before,
which happens every day,
which she does not notice.

ORPHEUS (1)

You walked in front of me,
pulling me back out
to the green light that had once
grown fangs and killed me.

I was obedient, but
numb, like an arm
gone to sleep; the return
to time was not my choice.

By then I was used to silence.
Though something stretched between us
like a whisper, like a rope:
my former name,
drawn tight.
You had your old leash
with you, love you might call it,
and your flesh voice.

Before your eyes you held steady
the image of what you wanted
me to become: living again.
It was this hope of yours that kept me following.

I was your hallucination, listening
and floral, and you were singing me:

already new skin was forming on me
within the luminous misty shroud
of my other body; already
there was dirt on my hands and I was thirsty.

I could see only the outline
of your head and shoulders,
black against the cave mouth,
and so could not see your face
at all, when you turned

and called to me because you had
already lost me. The last
I saw of you was a dark oval.
Though I knew how this failure
would hurt you, I had to
fold like a grey moth and let go.

You could not believe I was more than your echo.

EURYDICE

He is here, come down to look for you.
It is the song that calls you back,
a song of joy and suffering
equally: a promise:
that things will be different up there
than they were last time.

You would rather have gone on feeling nothing,
emptiness and silence; the stagnant peace
of the deepest sea, which is easier
than the noise and flesh of the surface.

You are used to these blanched dim corridors,
you are used to the king
who passes you without speaking.

The other one is different
and you almost remember him.
He says he is singing to you
because he loves you,

not as you are now,
so chilled and minimal: moving and still
both, like a white curtain blowing
in the draft from a half-opened window
beside a chair on which nobody sits.

He wants you to be what he calls real.
He wants you to stop light.
He wants to feel himself thickening
like a treetrunk or a haunch
and see blood on his eyelids
when he closes them, and the sun beating.

This love of his is not something
he can do if you aren't there,
but what you knew suddenly as you left your body
cooling and whitening on the lawn

was that you love him anywhere,
even in this land of no memory,
even in this domain of hunger.
You hold love in your hand, a red seed
you had forgotten you were holding.

He has come almost too far.
He cannot believe without seeing,
and it's dark here.
Go back, you whisper,

but he wants to be fed again
by you. O handful of gauze, little
bandage, handful of cold
air, it is not through him
you will get your freedom.

THE ROBBER BRIDEGROOM

He would like not to kill. He would like
what he imagines other men have,
instead of this red compulsion. Why do the women
fail him and die badly? He would like to kill them gently,
finger by finger and with great tenderness, so that
at the end they would melt into him
with gratitude for his skill and the final pleasure
he still believes he could bring them
if only they would accept him,
but they scream too much and make him angry.
Then he goes for the soul, rummaging
in their flesh for it, despotic with self-pity,
hunting among the nerves and the shards
of their faces for the one thing
he needs to live, and lost
back there in the poplar and spruce forest
in the watery moonlight, where his young bride,
pale but only a little frightened,
her hands glimmering with his own approaching
death, gropes her way towards him
along the obscure path, from white stone
to white stone, ignorant and singing,
dreaming of him as he is.

LETTER FROM PERSEPHONE

This is for the left-handed mothers
in their fringed black shawls or flowered housecoats
of the 'forties, their pink mule slippers,
their fingers, painted red or splay-knuckled
that played the piano formerly.

I know about your houseplants
that always died, about your spread

thighs roped down and split
between, and afterwards
that struggle of amputees
under a hospital sheet that passed
for sex and was never mentioned,
your invalid mothers, your boredom,
the enraged sheen of your floors;
I know about your fathers
who wanted sons.

These are the sons
you pronounced with your bodies,
the only words you could
be expected to say,
these flesh stutters.

No wonder this one
is nearly mute, flinches when touched,
is afraid of caves
and this one threw himself at a train
so he could feel his own heartbeat
once anyway; and this one
touched his own baby gently
he thought, and it came undone;
and this one enters the trussed bodies
of women as if spitting.

I know you cry at night
and they do, and they are looking for you.

They wash up here, I get
this piece or that. It's a blood
puzzle.

It's not your fault
either, but I can't fix it.

HARVEST

The villagers are out hunting for you.
They have had enough of potions
for obtaining love: they do not want love
this year, the crops were scant, a bad wind
came with the fall mists and they want you.

Already they have burned your house,
broken your mirror
in which they used to glimpse over their shoulders
the crescent moon and the face
of the one desired,
kicked the charred bedding apart
looking for amulets, gutted your cats.

By night you walk in the fields, fending off
the voices that rustle in the air
around you, wading streams
to kill your smell,
or creep into the barns to steal milk
and the turnips the pigs eat.
By day you hide,
digging yourself in under the hedges,
your dress becoming the colour of ashes.
Praying to the rain to save you.

Through the smooth grey tree-trunks there are fragments
of coats, the red wool
sashes, whistles rallying the dogs,
drifting towards you through the leaves falling
like snow, like pestilence.

Of the men who will stand around
the peeled stake dug into a pit,
bundles of sticks and dried reeds piled
nearby, the mud caked on their bootsoles,
crooking their fingers to ward you off,
at the same time joking about
your slashed breasts and the avid
heat to come, there is not one

who has not run his hands over your skin
in stealth, yours or your shadow's,

not one who has not straddled you
in the turned furrows, begging for increase.

What you will see: the sun, for the last time.
The tree-strewn landscape gathering itself
around you; the blighted meadows.
The dark ring of men whose names
you know, and their bodies
you remember as nameless, luminous.
The children, on the edges

of the circle, twisting on the ground,
arms uplifted and spread, mouths open, playing
at being you. In the distance, the wives
in their flowered shawls and thick decorous
skirts, hurrying from their houses
with little pierced copper
bowls in their hands, as if offering food
at a feast, bringing the embers.

NO NAME

This is the nightmare you now have frequently:
that a man will come to your house at evening
with a hole in him — you place it
in the chest, on the left side — and blood leaking out
onto the wooden door as he leans against it.

He is a man in the act of vanishing
one way or another.
He wants you to let him in.
He is like the soul of a dead
lover, come back to the surface of the earth
because he did not have enough of it and is still hungry

but he is far from dead. Though the hair
lifts on your arms and cold
air flows over your threshold
from him, you have never
seen anyone so alive

as he touches, just touches your hand
with his left hand, the clean
one, and whispers *Please*
in any language.

You are not a doctor or anything like it.
You have led a plain life
which anyone looking would call blameless.
On the table behind you
there are bread on a plate, fruit in a bowl.
There is one knife. There is one chair.

It is spring, and the night wind
is moist with the smell of turned loam
and the early flowers;
the moon pours out its beauty
which you see as beauty finally,
warm and offering everything.
You have only to take.
In the distance you hear dogs barking.

Your door is either half open
or half closed.
It stays that way and you cannot wake.

ORPHEUS (2)

Whether he will go on singing
or not, knowing what he knows
of the horror of this world:

He was not wandering among meadows
all this time. He was down there
among the mouthless ones, among
those with no fingers, those
whose names are forbidden,
those washed up eaten into
among the grey stones
of the shore where nobody goes
through fear. Those with silence.

He has been trying to sing
love into existence again
and he has failed.

Yet he will continue
to sing, in the stadium
crowded with the already dead
who raise their eyeless faces
to listen to him; while the red flowers
grow up and splatter open
against the walls.

They have cut off both his hands
and soon they will tear
his head from his body in one burst
of furious refusal.
He foresees this. Yet he will go on
singing, and in praise.
To sing is either praise
or defiance. Praise is defiance.

READING A POLITICAL THRILLER
BESIDE A REMOTE LAKE
IN THE CANADIAN SHIELD

I give you yourself, or
me, back propped
against a rock, with a skin of brown lichen
edible in extreme need.
This rock came straight up out of the earth
which was not earth then.
It is much older
than these words, or the hands
that hold them here, too close
to your eyes, this paper
world which is the real world
also: intricate wire
devices, lies, men who pretend
to kill because they must,

blowing each other up
in the best of causes,
and the refugees who die and refuse
to forget, and die once more.
Almost you envy
their hatred and ferocity,
which at least make everything clear,
narrow a landscape down
to a blunt point: target and power.

Is this plot more important
than the sunset?
Which is thick as blood but nothing
of the kind:
tonight flamingo, melting
into the water like love, true
and fervent: motif
hackneyed as bravery,
which criminals practise also.

Is it viciousness of the genes
that drives us on,
the quest for protein?
Starvation too is a creed.

There's a moon. What could be purer?
In this light, hard to believe
in any motive.
The trees go on and on.
Granite against your flesh, your flesh
empty and peaceful. Too dark to read.

In the closed book, the rivals
are at each others' throats
for a few miles of stone, a village
you wouldn't look twice at.

For them it is not a story.
This lake is dying.
Light the lamp,
pull the forest up over your body.
Sleep while you can.

III

THE WORDS CONTINUE
THEIR JOURNEY

Do poets really suffer more
than other people? Isn't it only
that they get their pictures taken
and are seen to do it?
The loony bins are full of those
who never wrote a poem.
Most suicides are not
poets: a good statistic.

Some days though I want, still,
to be like other people;
but then I go and talk with them,
these people who are supposed to be
other, and they are much like us,
except that they lack the sort of thing
we think of as a voice.
We tell ourselves they are fainter
than we are, less defined,
that they are what we are defining,
that we are doing them a favour,
which makes us feel better.
They are less elegant about pain than we are.

But look, I said *us*. Though I may hate your guts
individually, and want never to see you,
though I prefer to spend my time
with dentists because I learn more,
I spoke of us as *we*, I gathered us
like the members of some doomed caravan

which is how I see us, travelling together,
the women veiled and singly, with that inturned
sight and the eyes averted,
the men in groups, with their moustaches
and passwords and bravado

in the place we're stuck in, the place we've chosen,
a pilgrimage that took a wrong turn

somewhere far back and ended
here, in the full glare
of the sun, and the hard red-black shadows
cast by each stone, each dead tree lurid
in its particulars, its doubled gravity, but floating
too in the aureole of *stone*, of *tree*,

and we're no more doomed really than anyone, as we go
together, through this moon terrain
where everything is dry and perishing and so
vivid, into the dunes, vanishing out of sight,
vanishing out of the sight of each other,
vanishing even out of our own sight,
looking for water.

A PAINTING OF ONE
LOCATION ON THE PLAIN

It's a journey with no end
in sight, and no end
after all; this place
is merely an oasis

which you can see as temporary,
a one-night stand,
if permanence makes you nervous.

There's nothing for us to do
apart from what is needed
to keep life going:
we eat, we drink, we lie down
together; if you want more,
there's the sky to admire,
serene as the evening before a war,
a few dry trees
and the vacancy of the desert

where tomorrow we will go out again
to make tracks in the sand
the wind will cover soon enough,

along with the bones
we also can't help making.

You could be sad because there isn't more,
or happy because there is
at least this much.

The sun's too hot, the water's poor,
the food is minimal, and I still
believe in free will:

the feast we're eating
in this golden haze of dust
is either a dead animal
or a blessing

or both. Take your life in your hands,
watch how it runs through your fingers
like sand or your own blood
into the ground you stand on

which is covered with stones and hard
and cloudy and endless as heaven.

Now you know where you are.

THE SKELETON,
NOT AS AN IMAGE OF DEATH

Your flesh moves under my fingers

and I remember *flesh* and *fingers*, as a child holding
the head of a flashlight cupped in my fist
in a dark room, seeing with such delight
the outlines of my own hand's
lucent skeleton, swathed in the red glow
of the blood clouded within

and this is how I hold
you: not as body,

as in planetary,
as in thing, bulk, object
but as a quickening,

a disturbance of the various
darknesses within my arms
like an eddy in the moonlit
lake where a fish moves unseen.

We rot inside, the doctor
said. To put a hand on another
is to touch death,
no doubt. Though there is also

this nebulous mist of interstellar
dust snagged by the gravity
of a few bones, mine,
but luminous:

even in the deep subarctic
of space beyond meaning, even among
the never alive, to approach
is to shine.

I hold you as I hold
water, swimming.

SUMACS

*

At night I leave food out
on a white plate, milk in a white cup
and sit waiting, in the kitchen chair
beside last month's newspapers
and the worn coat leaning against
the wall: the shape of you left in the air,
time seeping out of it.
In the morning nothing has been touched
again. It is the wrong time of year.

*

Later, the days of the week unhook
from their names; the weeks unhook.
I do not lock the door
any more, but go outside and down
the bank, among the sumacs
with their tongues of dried blood
which have stopped speaking, to the pond
with its blackening water
and the one face wavering in it

wordless. Heaviness of the flesh infests me,
my skin that holds me in its nets;
I wish to change shape, as you have done
and be what you are

but that would be untrue also.

*

I lie on the damp yellowed grass bent
as if someone has been walking here
and press my head to the ground.

Come back, I tell you.
It becomes April.

If the daffodil would shed its paper
husk and fold back into its teardrop
and then down into the earth
into its cold onion
and into sleep. The one place I can still meet you.

*

Grief is to want more.
What use is moonlight?
I reach into it, fingers open,
and my hand is silvered
and blessed, and comes back to me holding nothing.

A BOAT

Evening comes on and the hills thicken;
red and yellow bleaching out of the leaves.
The chill pines grow their shadows.

Below them the water stills itself,
a sunset shivering in it.
One more going down to join the others.

Now the lake expands
and closes in, both.

The blackness that keeps itself
under the surface in daytime
emerges from it like mist
or as mist.

Distance vanishes, the absence
of distance pushes against the eyes.

There is no seeing the lake,
only the outlines of the hills
which are almost identical,

familiar to me as sleep,
shores unfolding upon shores
in their contours of slowed breathing.

It is touch I go by,
the boat like a hand feeling
through shoals and among
dead trees, over the boulders
lifting unseen, layer
on layer of drowned time falling away.

This is how I learned to steer
through darkness by no stars.

To be lost is only a failure of memory.

A BLAZED TRAIL

(i)

It was the pain of trees
that made this trail;
the fluid cut flesh of them only
partially hardened.
It is their scars that mark the way
we follow to the place where
the vista has closed over
and there is no more foresight.

(ii)

To blaze is also to burn.
All pathways through this burning
forest open in front of you and close
behind until you lose them.

This is the forest of lost things:
abandoned boulders. Burrows.
Roots twisted into the rock.
A toad in its cool
aura; an earthstar, splayed open
and leathery, releasing dust.
None of these things knows it is lost.

(iii)

We've come to a sunset, red and autumnal,
another burial. Although it is not
autumn, the wind has that chill.
Slight wind of a door closing.
The final slit of the old moon.

(iv)

I pick my way slowly
with you through the blazed forest,
scar by scar, back through
history, following the rule:

To recover what you have lost,
retrace your footsteps to the moment
at which you lost it. It will be there.

Here is the X in time.
When I am alone finally
my shadow and my own name
will come back to me.

(v)

I kneel and dig with my knifeblade
in the soil and find nothing.
I have forgotten what I hid here.

It must be the body of clear air
I left here carefully buried
and thought I could always
come back to and inhabit.

I thought I could be with myself only.
I thought I could float.
I thought I would always have a choice.
Now I am earthbound.
An incarnation.

(vi)

This is the last walk
I will take with you in your absence.

Your skin flares where I touch it,
then fades and the wood solidifies
around you. We are this momentary.

How much I love you.
I would like to be wise and calm.

I would make you eternal,
I would hold back your death if I could,
but where would you be without it?

We can live forever,
but only from time to time.

(vii)

Now we have reached the rocky point
and the shore, and the sky is deepening,
though the water still holds light

and gives it out, like fumes
or like fire. I wait, listening to that
place where a sound should be
and is not,
which is not my heart
or yours, which is darker
and more solitary,
which approaches. Which is the sound
the earth will make for itself
without us. A stone echoing a stone.
The pines rushing motionless.

INTERLUNAR

Darkness waits apart from any occasion for it;
like sorrow it is always available.
This is only one kind,

the kind in which there are stars
above the leaves, brilliant as steel nails
and countless and without regard.

We are walking together
on dead wet leaves in the intermoon
among the looming nocturnal rocks
which would be pinkish grey
in daylight, gnawed and softened
by moss and ferns, which would be green,
in the musty fresh yeast smell
of trees rotting, each returning
itself to itself

and I take your hand, which is the shape a hand
would be if you existed truly.
I wish to show you the darkness
you are so afraid of.

Trust me. This darkness
is a place you can enter and be
as safe in as you are anywhere;
you can put one foot in front of the other
and believe the sides of your eyes.
Memorize it. You will know it
again in your own time.
When the appearances of things have left you,
you will still have this darkness.
Something of your own you can carry with you.

We have come to the edge:
the lake gives off its hush;
in the outer night there is a barred owl
calling, like a moth
against the ear, from the far shore
which is invisible.
The lake, vast and dimensionless,
doubles everything, the stars,
the boulders, itself, even the darkness
that you can walk so long in
it becomes light.

NEW POEMS

1985–1986

AGEING FEMALE POET SITS
ON THE BALCONY

The front lawn is littered with young men
who want me to pay attention to them
not to their bodies and their freshly-
washed cotton skins, not to their enticing
motifs of bulb and root, but
to their poems. In the back yard
on the other hand are the older men
who want me to pay attention to their
bodies. Ah men,
why do you want
all this attention?
I can write poems for myself, make
love to a doorknob if absolutely
necessary. What do you have to offer me
I can't find otherwise
except humiliation? Which I no longer
need. I gather
dust, for practice, my attention
wanders like a household pet
once leashed, now
out on the prowl, an animal
neither dog nor cat, unique
and hairy, snuffling
among the damp leaves at the foot
of the hedge, among the afterbloom
of irises which melt like blue and purple
ice back into air; hunting for something
lost, something to eat or love, among
the twists of earth,
among the glorious bearclaw sun-
sets, evidence
of the red life that is leaking
out of me into time, which become
each night more final.

PORCUPINE TREE

A porcupine tree is always
dead or half dead with chewed core
and mangy bark. Droppings drool down it.
In winter you can see it clear:
shreds of wood, porcupine piss
as yellow ice, toothwork, trails to and from
waddling in the snow. In summer you smell it.
This tree
is bigger than the other trees,
frowsy as my
room or my vocabulary.
It does not make
leaves much any more,
only porcupines and porcupines,
fat, slow and lazy,
each one a low note, the longest string
on a cello,
or like turning over in bed
under the eiderdown in spring,
early before the leaves are out;
sunlight too hot on you through the window,
your head sodden with marshy dreams
or like a lungfish burrowed
into mud. Oh pigsheart. Oh luxury.

I'll come around at night
and gnaw the salt off your hands,
eat toilet seats and axe handles.
That is my job in life: to sniff
your worn skin music,
to witness the border
between flesh and the inert,
lick up dried blood
soaked into the grain,
the taste of mortality in the wood.

AGEING FEMALE POET READS LITTLE MAGAZINES

Amazingly young beautiful woman poets
with a lot of hair falling down around
their faces like a bad ballet,
their eyes oblique over their cheekbones;
they write poems like blood in a dead person
that comes out black, or at least deep
purple, like smashed grapes.
Perhaps I was one of them once.
Too late to remember
the details, the veils.
If I were a man I would want to console them,
and would not succeed.

PORCUPINE MEDITATION

I used to have tricks, dodges, a whole sackful.
I could outfox anyone,
double back, cover my tracks,
walk backwards, the works.
I left it somewhere, that knack
of running, that good luck.

Now I have only
one trick left: head down, spikes out,
brain tucked in.
I can roll up:
thistle as animal, a flower of quills,
that's about it.

I lie in the grass and watch the sunlight pleating
the skin on the backs of my hands
as if I were a toad, squashed and drying.

I don't even wade through spring water
to cover my scent.
I can't be bothered.

I squat and stink, thinking:
peace and quiet are worth something.
Here I am, dogs,
nose me over,
go away sneezing, snouts full of barbs
hooking their way to your brain.
Now you've got some
of my pain. Much good may it do you.

AGEING FEMALE POET ON LAUNDRY DAY

I prop up my face and go out, avoiding the sunlight,
keeping away from the curve where the burnt road
touches the sky.
Whatever exists at the earth's centre will get me
sooner or later. Sooner. Than I think.
That core of light squeezed tight
and shut, dense as a star, as molten
mirrors. Dark red and heavy. Slab at the butcher's.
Already it's dragging me down. already
I become shorter, infinitesimally.
The bones of my legs thicken — that's first —
contract, like muscles.
After that comes the frailty, a dry wind blowing
inside my body,
scouring me from within, as if I were
a fossil, the soft parts eaten away.
Soon I will turn to calcium. It starts with the heart.

I do a lot of washing. I wash everything.
If I could only get this clean once, before I die.

To see God, they told me, you do not go
into the forest or city; not the meadow,
the seashore even unless it is cold.
You go to the desert.
You think of sand.

NIGHTSHADE ON THE WAY TO SCHOOL

Nightshade grows more densely than most weeds:
in the country of burdock and random stones,
rooted in undersides of damp logs,
leaf mould, worm castings.
Dark foliage, strong tendrils, the flowers purple
for mourning but with a centre
so yellow I thought *buttercup* or *adder*,
the berries red, translucent,
like the eggs of an unknown moth,
feather-soft, nocturnal.
Belladonna was its name, *beautiful lady*.
Its other name was *deadly*.
If you ate it it would stop your heart,
you would sleep forever. I was told that.
Sometimes it was used for healing,
or in the eyes. I learned that later.

I had to go down the mud path to the ravine,
the wooden bridge across it rotting,
walk across it, from good
board to good board,
level with the tips of the trees.
Birds I don't remember.
On the other side the thicket of nightshade
where cats hunted, leaving their piss:
a smell of ammonia and rust, some dead thing.
All this in sunshine.

At that time I did well, my fingers
were eaten down to the blood.
They never healed.
The word *Nightshade* a shadow,
the colour of a recurring dream
in which you cannot see colour.
Porridge, worn underwear, wool
stockings, my fault. Not purple: some
other colour. Sick
outside in a snowbank.

I dreamed of falling from the bridge,
one hand holding on, unable to call.
In other dreams, I could step into the air.
It was not flying. I never flew.

Now some years I cross the new bridge,
concrete, the path white gravel.
The old bridge is gone,
the nightshade has been cut down.
The nightshade spreads and thickens
where it always was,
at this season the red berries.
You would be tempted to eat them
if you did not know better.
Also the purple flowers.

AN ANGEL

I know what the angel of suicide looks like. I have seen her several times. She's around.

She's nothing like the pictures of angels you run across here and there, the ones in classical paintings, with their curls and beautiful eyelashes, or the ones on Christmas cards, all cute or white. Much is made, in these pictures, of the feet, which are always bare, I suppose to show that angels do not need shoes: walkers on nails and live coals all of them, aspirin hearts, dandelion-seed heads, airbodies.

Not so the angel of suicide, who is dense, heavy with anti-matter, a dark star. But despite the differences, she does have something in common with those others. All angels are messengers, and so is she; which isn't to say that all messages are good. The angels vary according to what they have to say: the angel of blindness for instance, the angel of lung cancer, the angel of seizures, the destroying angel. The latter is also a mushroom.

(Snow angels, you've seen them: the cold blank shape of yourself, the outline you once filled. They too are messengers, they come from the future. This is what you will be, they say; perhaps what you are: no more than the way light falls across a given space.)

Angels come in two kinds: the others, and those who fell. The angel of suicide is one of those who fell, down through the atmosphere to the earth's surface. Or did she jump? With her you have to ask.

Anyway, it was a long fall. From the friction of the air her face melted off like the skin of a meteor. That is why the angel of suicide is so smooth. She has no face to speak of. She has the face of a grey egg. Noncommittal; though the shine of the fall still lingers.

They said, the pack of them, I will not serve. The angel of suicide is one of those: a rebellious waitress. Rebellion, that's what she has to offer, to you, when you see her beckoning to you from outside the window, fifty storeys up, or the edge of the bridge, or holding something out to you, some emblem of release, soft chemical, quick metal.

Wings, of course. You wouldn't believe a thing she said if it weren't for the wings.

MOTHERS

How much havoc this woman spills
out of herself into us
merely by being
unhappy with such finality:

The mothers rise up in us,
rustling, uttering cooing
sounds, their hands moving
into our hands, patting anything
smooth again. Her deprived eyes and deathcamp
shoulders. There there

we say, bringing
bright things in desperation:
a flower? We make
 dolls of other people and offer
them to her. Have him, we say,
what about her? Eat their heads off
for all we care, but stop crying.

She half sits in the bed, shaking
her head under the cowl of hair.
Nothing will do, ever.

She discards us, crumples down
into the sheets, twisting around
that space we can never
hope to fill,
hugging her true mother,
the one who left her here
not among us:
hugging her darkness.

SHE

The snake hunts and sinews
his way along and is not his own
idea of viciousness. All he wants is
a fast grab, with fur and a rapid
pulse, so he can take that fluttering
and make it him, do a transfusion.
They say *whip* or *rope* about him, but this
does not give the idea; nor
phallus, which has no bones,
kills nothing and cannot see.
The snake sees red, like a hand held
above sunburn. Zeroes in,
which means, aims for the round egg
with nothing in it but blood.
If lucky, misses the blade
slicing light just behind him.
He's our idea of a bad time, we are his.
I say *he* out of habit. It could be *she*.

WEREWOLF MOVIES

Men who imagine themselves covered with fur and sprouting
fangs, why do they do that? Padding among wet
moonstruck treetrunks crouched on all fours, sniffing
the mulch of sodden leaves, or knuckling
their brambly way, arms dangling like outsized
pyjamas, hair all over them, noses and lips
sucked back into their faces, nothing left of their kindly
smiles but yellow eyes and a muzzle. This gives them
pleasure, they think they'd be
more animal. Could then freely growl, and tackle
women carrying groceries, opening
their doors with keys. Freedom would be
bared ankles, the din of tearing: rubber, cloth,
whatever. Getting down to basics. Peel, they say
to strippers, meaning: take off the skin.
A guzzle of flesh
dogfood, ears in the bowl. But
no animal does that: couple and kill,
or kill first: rip up its egg, its future.
No animal eats its mate's throat, except
spiders and certain insects, when it's the protein
male who's gobbled. Why do they have this dream then?
Dress-ups for boys, some last escape
from having to be lawyers? Or a
rebellion against the mute
resistance of objects: reproach of the
pillowcase big with pillow, the tea-
cosy swollen with its warm
pot, not soft as it looks but hard
as it feels, round tummies of saved string in the top
drawer tethering them down. What joy, to smash the
tyranny of the doorknob, sink your teeth
into the inert defiant eiderdown with matching
spring-print queensized sheets and listen to her
scream. Surrender.

MEN AT SEA

You can come to the end of talking, about women, talking. In restaurants, cafes, kitchens, less frequently in bars or pubs, about relatives, relations, relationships, illnesses, jobs, children, men; about nuance, hunch, intimation, intuition, shadow; about themselves and each other; about what he said to her and she said to her and she said back; about what they feel.

Something more definite, more outward then, some action, to drain the inner swamp, sweep the inner fluff out from under the inner bed, harden the edges. Men at sea, for instance. Not on a submarine, too claustrophobic and smelly, but something more bracing, a tang of salt, cold water, all over your calloused body, cuts and bruises, hurricanes, bravery and above all no women. Women are replaced by water, by wind, by the ocean, shifting and treacherous, a man has to know what to do, to navigate, to sail, to bail, so reach for the How To book, and out here it's what he said to him, or didn't say, a narrowing of the eyes, sizing the bastard up before the pounce, the knife to the gut, and here comes a wave, hang on to the shrouds, all teeth grit, all muscles bulge together. Or sneaking along the gangway, the passageway, the right of way, the milky way, in the dark, your eyes shining like digital wristwatches, and the bushes, barrels, scuppers, ditches, filthy with enemies, and you on the prowl for adrenalin and loot. Corpses of your own making deliquesce behind you as you reach the cave, abandoned city, safe, sliding panel, hole in the ground, and rich beyond your wildest dreams!

What now? Spend it on some woman, in a restaurant. And there I am, back again at the eternal table, which exists so she can put her elbows on it, over a glass of wine, while he says. What does he say? He says the story of how he got here, to her. She says: But what did you feel?

And his eyes roll wildly, quick as a wink he tries to think of something else, a cactus, a porpoise, never give yourself away, while the seductive waves swell the carpet beneath the feet and the wind freshens among the tablecloths. They're all around her, she can see it now, one per woman per table. Men, at sea.

ADVENTURE STORY

This is a story told by our ancestors, and those before them. It is not just a story, but something they once did, and at last there is proof.

Those who are to go must prepare first. They must be strong and well-nourished and they must possess also a sense of purpose, a faith, a determination to persevere to the end, because the way is long and arduous and there are many dangers.

At the right time they gather together in the appointed place. Here there is much confusion and milling around, as yet there is no order, no groups of sworn companions have separated themselves from the rest. The atmosphere is tense, anticipation stirs among them, and now, before some are ready, the adventure has been launched. Through the dark tunnel, faintly lit with lurid gleams of reddish light, shoots the intrepid band, how many I cannot say; only that there are many: a band now, for all are headed in the same direction. The safety of the home country falls behind, the sea between is crossed more quickly than you can think, and now they are in alien territory, a tropical estuary with many coves and hidden bays. The water is salt, the vegetation Amazonian, the land ahead shrouded and obscure, thickened with fog. Monstrous animals, or are they fish, lurk here, pouncing upon the stragglers, slaying many. Others are lost, and wander until they weaken and perish in misery.

Now the way narrows, and those who have survived have reached the gate. It is shut, but they try one password and then another, and look! the gate has softened, melted, turned to jelly, and they pass through. Magic still works; an unseen force is on their side. Another tunnel; here they must crowd together, swimming upstream, between shores curving and fluid as lava, helping one another. Only together can they succeed.

(You may think I'm talking about male bonding, or war, but no: half of these are female, and they swim and help and sacrifice their lives in the same way as the rest.)

And now there is a widening out, and the night sky arches above them, or are we in outer space and all the rocket movies you've ever seen? It's still warm, whatever, and the team, its numbers sadly diminished, forges onward, driven by what? Greed for treasure, desire for a new home, worlds to conquer, a raid on an enemy citadel, quest for the grail? Now it is each alone, and the mission becomes a race which only one may win, as, ahead of them, vast and luminous, the longed-for, the loved planet swims into view, like a moon, a sun, an image of God, round and perfect. A target.

Farewell, my comrades, my sisters! You have died that I may live! I alone will enter the garden, while you must wilt and shrivel in outer darkness. So saying—and you know, because now this is less like a story than a memory—the victorious one reaches the immense perimeter and is engulfed in the soft pink atmosphere of paradise, sinks, enters, casts the imprisoning skin of the self, merges, disappears . . . and the world slowly explodes, doubles, revolves, changes for ever, and there, in the desert heaven, shines a fresh-laid star, exile and promised land in one, harbinger of a new order, a new birth, possibly holy; and the animals will be named again.

(You switch off the television. Imagine that! Conception, live on the screen, filmed with miniature cameras. Now how in hell did they do it, you wonder. Lasers, they say; but who was watching, and where were they standing, and what next?)

HOW TO TELL ONE COUNTRY FROM ANOTHER

Whether it is possible to become lost.

Whether one tree looks like another.
Whether there is water all around
the edges or not. Whether
there are edges or whether
there are just insects.

Whether the insects bite,
whether you would die
from the bites of the insects.
Whether you would die.

Whether you would die for your country.
Whether anyone in the country would die for your country.
Let's be honest here.
A layer of snow, a layer of granite, a layer of snow.
What you think lies under the snow.
What you think lies.

Whether you think white on white is a state of mind
or blue on blue or green on green.
Whether you think there is a state,
of mind.

How many clothes you have to take off
before you can make love.
This I think is important:
the undoing of buttons, the gradual shedding
of one colour after another. It leads
to the belief that what you see is not
what you get.

Whether there are preliminaries,
hallways, vestibules,
basements, furnaces,
chesterfields, silences
between sentences, between pieces
of furniture, parasites in your eyes,
drinkeable water.

Whether there has ever been
an invading army.
Whether, if there were an invading army,
you would collaborate.
Poor boy, you'd say, he looks cold
standing out there, and he's only twenty.
From his point of view this must be hell.

A fur coat is what he needs,
a cup of tea, a cup of coffee,
a warm body.
Whether on the contrary
you'd slit his throat in his sleep
or in yours. I ask you.

So, you are a nice person.
You would behave well.
What you mean by behaving well.
When the outline of a man
whose face you cannot see
appears at your bedroom window,
whether you would shoot.
If you had a gun, that is.
Whether you would have a gun.
It goes on.

164

MACHINE. GUN. NEST.

The blood goes through your neck veins with a noise they call singing.
Time shatters like bad glass; you are this pinpoint of it.

Your feet rotting inside your boots, the skin of your chest
festering under the zippers, the waterproof armour,

you sit here, on the hill, a vantage point, at this X or scuffling
in the earth, which they call a nest. Who chose that word?

Whatever you are you are not an egg, or a bird either.
Vipers perhaps is what was meant. Who cares now?

That is the main question: who cares. Not these pieces of paper
from somewhere known as *home* you fold, unread, in your pocket.

Each landscape is a state of mind, he once told me:
mountains for awe and remoteness, meadows for calm and the steam

of the lulled senses. But some views are slippery.
This place is both beautiful as the sun and full of menace:

dark green, with now and then a red splotch, like a punctured
vein, white like a flare; stench of the half-eaten.
Look at it carefully, see what it hides, or it will burst in your head.

If you lose your nerve you may die, if you don't lose it
you may die anyway, the joke goes. What is your nerve?

It is turning the world flat, the moon to a disc you could aim at,
popping the birds off the fence wire. Delight in accuracy,

no attention paid to results, dead singing, the smear of feathers.
You know you were more than that, but best to forget it.

There's no slack time for memory here; when you can, you plunge
into some inert woman as into a warm bath; for a moment
comforting, and of no consequence, like sucking your thumb.

No woman can imagine this. What you do to them
is therefore incidental, and also your just reward,

though sometimes, in a gap in the action, there's a space
for the concepts of *sister*, *mother*. Like folded laundry. They come and go.

But stick your hand up a woman, alive or freshly-
dead, it is much like a gutted chicken:
giblets, a body cavity. Killing can be

merely a kind of impatience, at the refusal
of this to mean anything to you. He told me that.

You wanted to go in sharp and clean with a sword,
do what they once called battle. Now you just want your life.

There's not much limit to what you would do to get it.
Justice and mercy are words that happen in cool rooms, elsewhere.

Are you your brother's keeper? Yes or no, depending
what clothes he has on, what hair. There is more than one brother.

What you need to contend with now is the hard Easter-
eggshell blue of the sky, that shows you too clearly

the mass of deep green trees leaning slowly towards you
as if on the verge of speech, or annunciation.

More likely some break in the fabric of sight, or a sad mistake
you will hear about in the moment you make it. Some glint of reflected lig

That whir in the space where your left hand was is not singing.
Death is the bird that hatches, is fed, comes flying.

THE REST

The rest of us watch from beyond the fence
as the woman moves with her jagged stride
into her pain as if into a slow race.
We see her body in motion
but hear no sounds, or we hear
sounds but no language; or we know
it is not a language we know
yet. We can see her clearly
but for her it is running in black smoke.
The clusters of cells in her swelling
like porridge boiling, and bursting,
like grapes, we think. Or we think of
explosions in mud; but we know nothing.
All around us the trees
and the grasses light up with forgiveness,
so green and at this time
of the year healthy.
We would like to call something
out to her. Some form of cheering.
There is pain but no arrival at anything.

ANOTHER ELEGY

Strawberries, pears, fingers, the eyes
of snails: the other shapes water
takes. Even leaves are liquid
arrested. To die
is to dry, lose juice,
the sweet pulp sucked out. To enter
the time of rind and stone.

Your clothes hang shrivelling
in the closet, your other body once
filled with your breath.
When I say *body*, what
is that a word for?
Why should the word *you*

remain attached to that suffering?
Wave upon wave, as we say.

I think of your hair burning
first, a scant minute
of halo; later, an afterglow
of bone, red slash of sunset.
The body a cinder or luminescent
saint, or Turner seascape.

Fine words, but why do I want
to tart up death?
Which needs no decoration,
which is only a boat,
plain and wooden
and ordinary, without eyes
painted on it,
sightless and hidden
in fog and going somewhere
else. Away from the shore.

My dear, my voyager, my scant handful
of ashes: I'd scatter you
if I could, this way, on the river.
A wave is neither form
nor energy. Both. Neither.

GALIANO COAST: FOUR ENTRANCES

i

The arbutus trees, with their bark like burned skin
that has healed, enclosing someone's real arms
in the moment of reaching, but not towards you:

you know they are paying no attention
to you and your failed love and equivocation.

Why do you wish to be forgiven by them?

Yet you are, and you breathe in,
and the new moon sheds grace without intention.

ii

You lie on your stomach
looking down through a crack between rocks:

the seaweed with its bladders and hairs,
the genital bodies hinted
by the pink flanges of limpets,
five starfish, each thickened purple arm
a drowning tongue,
the sea's membrane, with its wet shine
and pulse, and no promise.

There is no future,
really there is none
and no salvation

To know this is salvation

iii

Where the rock stops upland, thistles burning
at the tips, leaving their white ash

A result of the sun, this pentecost
and conflagration.

Light flares up off the tidepool
where the barnacles grasp at the water
each with its one skeletal hand
which is also a frond

which is also a tongue
which is also a flame
you are praised by

iv

Sandrock the colour of erosion,
pushed by the wind
into gills and clefts
and heavy folds like snow melting
or the crease of a doubled arm

There ought to be caves here

The sunlight
slides over the body like pollen

A door is about to open
onto paradise. Onto a beach like this one,

exactly like it, down to each thistle,
down to the red halfcrab eaten on the sand,
down to the rubber glove
gone white and blinded,
wedged in and stranded by the tide

down to the loss because you
can never truly be here.

Can this be paradise, with so much loss
in it?

      Paradise
is defined by loss.
                     Is loss.
Is.

SQUAW LILIES: SOME NOTES

Went up the steep stone hill, thinking,
My trick hip could fail me. Went up anyway
to see the flower with three names:
chocolate lilies, for the colour,
stink lilies for the smell, red meat going off,
squaw lilies. Thought what I would be like, falling.
Brain spilled on the rocks.
Said to her: never seen these before. Why squaw?
Oh, she said, something to do
with the smell.
When she said that I felt as if painted

naked on an off-blue sofa
by a bad expressionist, ochre
and dirty greens, lips thickened with yellow
pigment, a red-infected
crevice dividing the splayed legs.
Thought: this is what it is, to be part
of the landscape. Subject to
depiction. Thought:
release the lilies. They have nothing
to do with these names for them.
Not even lilies.
Went down the steep stone hill. Did not fall.

ST LAZARIUS

Short version: We go by boat to St. Lazarius. It's June and chilly.
We anchor, eat, wait for the tide to rise, land from a rubber
dinghy. We walk around, climb up, climb down. We get into
the boat and go back to the mainland.

Longer version:

Wave heave and yaw: the drone note in a lament
going on under the shining flourishes of the upper air.
Geology drifted past until we hit some of it:

an engraving—*Solitude*—from the last century,
rounded verticals, foliage, too much inky cross-hatch;
up close, hot basalt hitting the sea, splintering

into black rock, a fixed explosion ten thousand years long.
Above us the snub-winged puffins launching themselves
from cliffs plump with their burrows.

Someone threw up in a bucket. We ate buns and cheese,
waiting for tide-rise so we could scramble ashore
over the sea's edge, with its flags and slippery innards,
its khaki-coloured lungs, leathery bladders.

First thing: a feathery tidepool, pinkish and mauvish,
half-toned, its gills caressing the water,
purple starfish, a handful
of cow tongues splayed on the rock.

Walk up : high on the lava hills, small pools
of fresh water, outcrops of low stoneflowers,
Shooting Stars, Beach Strawberries,
cuticles of the bud pulled back, each colour
vivid as a scratch, roots clamped into the fissures.

Walk down: the inlet gravelled with rounded
cinders, hidden from all sides; the two crows, scorch-black,
who chased me away with their voices: raw! raw!
from the invisible egg at the living centre
of the space they considered theirs.

In the water-curved caves the murres groaning, sound of suffering,
which is not that but courtship or hunger. Guesswork.

Thickness is what I look for, layer on
layer, the bared rock fat with it,
gulls rising like shaken apple
petals, ammonia smell of guano,
the green anemone, its tentacles pulled in, pursed
like lemon-smeared lips against low tide; strange flesh, venusian anus.

Look what I did, just by calling it that.

Indian pipes, we say. Coming up through the soil
elsewhere, a silvery-white gleam under a leaf, like an
upturned eyeball. *Corpse plant* is the other name.

You see what can be done
with words, but why do we do it?
We want things to talk
with us, with our own words,
we are that stupid and lonely,

we think we can name things. Clubmoss,
lichen on dead tree, fungus,
names clumsy or brutal, cunt and fuck, pigshead, plughole,
cesspit, lousewart, slug on a leaf, spit, hate.

The names we make fall like soot, obscuring the light,
but porous, but misty: look, your hand goes right through them,

even the other names, Cosmos, Angel-fish, Jewel-
weed, or silver Honesty, or papery Everlasting,
even the fifty-two names for snow, and the nine for love.

This naming can go on, words coming out of you endlessly
into the air year after year until you are empty
and think nothing answers you, not in your own words,
only this grieving lament from the caves, bird-voice or sea together,
which has no meaning you can make out; which is not naming.

Here the text should say something
about the emptiness and the void behind things.
Absurdity means deafness, I was told early,
but this kind of silence does not mean failure to hear,
though what's being heard may not be our Adam-headed commands.

Empty of what? the sea says. What did you want instead
of the luminous *this is*, *this is*, *this is* of the waves?
Your sadness is yours. There is no void, it is not empty,

lightyears, the rasp of burnt-out gravel
across your hand, the licking starfish, the puke in the bucket, the snot-
coloured nodes of seaweed lapping the edges
of island upon island, the islands, the white noise of time
that lies between my saying and your hearing
this is, the radiant
absences between the stars: not.

THREE PRAISES

*

The dipper, small dust-coloured bird with robin
feet, walks on the stream bed
enclosed in its nimbus of silver
air, miraculous bubble, a non-miracle.
Who could have thought it? We think it now,
and liverwort on a dead log, earthstar,
hand, finger by finger.

*

For you, at last, I'd like to make
something uncomplicated; some neither god
nor goddess, not between, beyond
them; pinch it from dough,
bake it in the oven, a stone in its belly.
Stones lined up on the windowsill,
picked off some beach or other for being holy.

*

The hookworm, in the eye of
the universe, which is the unsteady gaze
of eternity maybe, is beloved. How could it not be,
living so blessed, in its ordained red meadows
of blood where it waves like a seaweed?
Praise be, it sings with its dracula mouth.
Praise be.

* * *

NOT THE MOON

What idiocy could transform the moon, that old sea-overgrown
skull seen from above, to a goddess of mercy?

You fish for the silver light, there on the quiet lake, so clear
to see; you plunge your hands into the water and come up empty.

Don't ask questions of stones. They will rightly ignore you,
they have shoulders but no mouths, their conversation is elsewhere.

Expect nothing else from the perfect white birdbones, picked clean
in the sedge in the cup of muskeg: you are none of their business.

Fresh milk in a glass on a plastic tray, a choice of breakfast
foods; we sit at the table, discussing the theories of tragedy.

The plump pink-faced men in the metal chairs at the edge of the golf course
adding things up, sunning themselves, adding things up.

The corpse, washed and dressed, beloved meat pumped full of chemicals
and burned, if turned back into money could feed two hundred.

Voluptuousness of the newspaper; scratching your back on the bad news;
furious anger in spring sunshine, a plate of fruit on the table.

Ask of the apple, crisp heart, ask the pear or suave banana
which necks got sucked, whose flesh got stewed, so we could love them.

The slug, a muscular jelly, slippery and luminous, dirty
eggwhite unrolling its ribbon of mucous—this too is delicious.

The oily slick, rainbow-coloured, spread on the sewage
flats in the back field is beautiful also

as is the man's hand cut off at the wrist and nailed to a treetrunk,
mute and imploring, as if asking for alms, or held up in warning.

Who knows what it tells you? It does not say, beg, *Have mercy*,
it is too late for that. Perhaps only, *I too was here once, where you are*.

The star-like flower by the path, by the ferns, in the rain-
forest, whose name I did not know, and the war in the jungle —

the war in the jungle, blood on the crushed ferns, whose name I do not
know, and the star-like flower grow out of the same earth

whose name I do not know. Whose name for itself I do not know.
Or much else, except that the moon is no goddess of mercy

but shines on us each damp warm night of her full rising
as if she were, and that is why we keep asking

the wrong questions, he said, of the wrong things. The questions of thing
                                   Ask the spider
what is the name of God, she will tell you: God is a spider.

Let the other moons pray to the moon. Oh Goddess of Mercy,
you who are not the moon, or anything we can see clearly,

we need to know each others' names and what we are asking.
Do not be any thing. Be the light we see by.